THE ILLUSTRATED BOOK OF SEXUAL RECORDS

THE
ILLUSTRATED
BOOK OF
SEXUAL
RECORDS

G.L. Simons

Bell Publishing Company
New York

This 1984 edition is published by Bell Publishing Company, by arrangement with Delilah Communications Ltd.

Manufactured in the United States of America

Conceived, edited and designed by Pilot Productions Limited, London.

Pictures: While every effort has been made to trace copyright sources, the publishers would be grateful to hear from any unacknowledged copyright holders.

Library of Congress Cataloging in Publication Data

Simons, G.L.
   The illustrated book of sexual records.

   Reprint. Originally published: New York : Delilah Books, 1983, c1982.
   1. Sex—Miscellanea. I. Title.
HQ25.S55 1984   306.7   84-6504
ISBN: 0-517-448998
h g f e d c b

Contents

Introduction

"In her abnormalities nature reveals her secrets" – GOETHE

Records, rarities, firsts ... the famous, the bizarre, the exceptional ... prodigies, freaks, anomalies – all such things arouse curiosity and wonder. In a related way, the English philosopher David Hume talked of man's "usual propensity towards the marvellous", a propensity which, in history, has cast the blind woman in the role of seer and turned albino children into gods.

Sex too has its perennial fascination for mankind. As sexual creatures, men and women are seldom indifferent to the promptings of libido. And yet the natural impulse can be distorted into personal bitterness and moral outrage: the wholesome preoccupation with sex has been represented as *deviant, misguided* and *unhealthy*. One thing emerges – sex is a potent force, too ingrained in the biology of life to be ignored. In simple indulgence, the power symbols, the urge to mate, sex makes its demands. It will not go away.

The idea of sexual "records" or "superlatives" links the evocative realms of the *exceptional* and the *erotic*: the sexual superlative has a double potency ...

Of the items set forth in the present volume four basic types may be identified –

    (1) matters of fact, well attested
    (2) matters of fact, poorly attested
    (3) matters of subjective evaluation
    (4) matters of fiction and legend

In the first class are the research findings of the best sexologists, the historical items scarcely open to doubt, and the simple truths laid up in common knowledge. In the second class are the factual claims made on a basis of poor documentation, anecdotal reference, and unsupported testimony. To the third class belong the personal assessments as to fame, pre-eminence, and what is bizarre, vicious, important, etc. And the fourth class says something of human dreams, fantasies and imaginings. I leave the reader to judge to which class any particular item belongs . . .

The superlatives have been selected partly on the basis of their inherent interest. In giving brief background details to many of the items it is also hoped that the reader will find "mini-profiles" of many areas impinging on sexual and erotic matters – animal and human physiology, evolution, psychology, deviancy, law, history, anthropology, custom, religion, superstition, contraception, fertility, sexology, art, literature, sculpture, photography, etc. In any event it is hoped that this catalogue of extremes, firsts, excesses, and the like will inform, enter-

tain, titillate, or simply amuse . . .

Part I

Human Physiology

Largest human penis

We all know that men are supposed to worry endlessly about penis size. In popular mythology a small organ is still thought to signal a totally inadequate lover. All the best books tell us that this idea is absurd but nonetheless the notion persists. What can we say of penis size? How big is the biggest? One problem is who is to do the measuring. If men measure their own organs they are likely to exaggerate the results: it is not an area in which there are abundant objective surveys. And women too may exaggerate the size of a particular penis in their acquaintance. Walter (of My Secret Life) demonstrated this clearly enough: a woman spoke of a penis as being 7 in. long or even more – yet the "very large penis" measured by Walter turned out to be significantly less than 7 in. According to Wardell B. Pomeroy, the Kinsey co-worker, the longest penis encountered was ten inches. This figure accords quite well with the results of the special Forum survey into penis size. In this careful and detailed survey, published in 1970, the largest penis was found to be $9\frac{1}{2}$ in. in erection, hardly able to compete with the vast organs of pornographic fiction. In an earlier inter-racial survey, Dr. Jacobus's 1935 publication – "L'Ethnologie du Sens Genitale", larger dimensions were recorded. In this survey, organs nearly 12 in. in length are reported. Of all penis sizes quoted in the literature the largest is unquestionably the 14 in. erect organ mentioned by Dr. David Reuben in "Everything You Always Wanted to Know About Sex". But as no source is quoted perhaps we should not take too much notice of this figure. The largest well-attested penises would seem to be between ten and twelve inches in the erect state.

Smallest human penis

Vast numbers of men – in one estimate the greater majority – think that they have a penis much below the average in size. Perhaps they should console themselves with the thought that many men have extremely diminutive organs. Pomeroy states that the smallest penis encountered in the Kinsey surveys was 1 in. long. In the Forum study the smallest erect penis was

"My agent told me never to accept small parts."

found to be 4.75 in. in length, quite large compared with many of the specimens that do exist. There are instances reported in the medical literature of penises that do not exceed 1 cm. in full erection: such organs are sometimes labelled with the appropriate term "micropenis". And even 1 cm. is not the smallest-sized penis known to medical researchers. There is a condition known as congenital hypoplasia, where the body of the penis is totally absent and the glans is attached to the pubic region. In one such reported case, with an effective penis of much less than 1 cm. in length, the testes and secondary sexual characteristics were found to be quite normal.

Largest penis by race

In the Dr. Jacobus survey definite penis size differences on a basis of race were detected. The largest Arab penises were found to be between eight and ten inches; but it was among the Muslim Sudanese that Jacobus found "the most developed phallus" – notably "one of the maximum dimensions, being nearly 12 in. in length, by a diameter of $2\frac{1}{4}$ in." The hardy researcher remarked that this was "a terrific machine" – "more likely the penis of a donkey than of a man." He concluded that the "Sudanese Negro possesses the

largest genital organ of all the races of mankind". In a less extensive survey, but equally interesting, Dr. Robert Chartham measured erect penises for groups of men of various nationalities. The largest organs for each nationality were as follows: English – $10\frac{1}{2}$ in.; West German – $8\frac{1}{4}$ in.; Negro – $7\frac{1}{2}$ in.; French – $7\frac{3}{4}$ in.; Danish – 8 in.; American – $7\frac{3}{4}$ in.; and Swedish – $7\frac{3}{4}$ in. The groups were small, ranging from only 9 to 121 individuals; nevertheless the data acquired are not without significance.

Smallest penis by race
In the Jacobus survey the Hindu man was reckoned to have a penis that only averaged around 4 inches, a much smaller figure than for the other races investigated. In the Chartham survey the smallest organs in the various nationality groups were as follows: English – $2\frac{3}{4}$ in.; West German – $3\frac{1}{2}$ in.; Negro – 4 in.; French $3\frac{1}{2}$ in.; Danish – 5 in.; American –

$3\frac{1}{2}$ in.; and Swedish – 5 in. As we have already suggested, with the groups being rather small no racial conclusions can be drawn.

Largest penis by sex offender class
The Kinsey group compiled data on penis size for the detailed report on sex offenders. Various classes of offenders were asked to estimate their penis length on the ventral surface from the abdomen to the tip of the penis. Penis lengths for various groups were found to average 6.3 to 6.5 in. It was found that only one group – "the aggressors v. minors" – reported an above-average length penis (around 6.75 in.). It was pointed out that contrary to expectation the estimated penis length of the exhibitionists was not unusual. These efforts represent one of the few attempts to discover correlations between penis size and types of sex offender. Some writers have seen fit, however, to remark **11**

on the penile characteristics of offenders. For instance it has been pointed out, by Colin Wilson in his "Origins of the Sexual Impulse" that the penis of the sexual murderer DeWitt Clinton Cook was "so tiny that he and his wife were forced to satisfy one another orally."

Most detailed record of phalli amputated in battle
In 1300 BC King Menephta returned to Karnak in Egypt after defeating the Libyans. As a mark of his success he brought with him more than 13,000 phalli taken from his defeated adversaries. On an ancient monument at Karnak details of his success are given:

Phalluses of Libyan generals	6
Phalluses cut off Libyans	6,359
Sirculians killed, phalluses cut off	222
Etruscans killed, phalluses cut off	542
Greeks killed, phalluses presented to the King	6,111

Largest human testicle
Testicles are much of muchness, varying in dimensions very little from man to man. One authority, T. H. Van de Velde in his "Ideal Marriage", puts the "mature testicle" at from 4 to $4\frac{1}{2}$ cm. long, and from 2 to $2\frac{4}{5}$ cm. broad. It is suggested that "at the utmost" the testicle does not exceed

5 cm. in length. This is probably true for healthy men, though venereal and other diseases can produce staggering results. In some maladies a testicle the size of a football is not unknown. One can only try to imagine the agony caused by elephantiasis and other conditions in which the testicles can swell to proportions vastly larger than the victim's head.

Heaviest human breasts
Many men, as we all know, are fascinated by massive breasts. Magazines cater specifically for such tastes and a number of strip-tease artists try hard to capitalise on their gigantic mammary apparatus (connoisseurs will recall the fifty-odd-inch busts of Big Julie and Big Bertha in the clubs). Zola wrote of Desire who kept a bar and a dance hall (was she based on fact?) – "she seemed so vast, with a pair of breasts each one of which required a man to embrace it. Rumour had it that nowadays she had to have two of her weekday lovers each night to cope with the job." In one recorded instance ("The Sexual Anatomy of Woman" by W. F. Benedict), a girl of fourteen had breasts weighing sixteen pounds; and in another case a woman of thirty had breasts weighing fifty-two pounds. As with the male sexual organs breasts are sometimes grossly enlarged by disease or some other unwelcome cause. For instance some

women have hyper-trophied breasts, sagging vastly and of quite giant proportions. An Abyssinian woman with this condition is shown by Mantegazza in his book, "The Sexual Relations of Mankind".

Most pendulous breasts by race

Breasts come in all shapes and sizes and hues. We have already noted some massive specimens: there are other ways in which breasts can be excessively dimensioned. They can, for instance, be extremely long, dangling like strips of skin. This occurs in a number of African tribes and can be common in both young and old women. It is not unknown for women to toss their breasts over their shoulders to keep them out of the way while working.

Least pendulous breasts by race

The smallest and least pendulous breasts are usually attributed to the Mongoloids. Among such people the women often-appear with an almost boyish slimness – and the vast mammaries favoured in other parts of the world would be regarded as monstrous deformities.

Most capacious human vagina

The human vagina, when not engaged in coitus, is often much smaller than the local penis. The vaginal tissue, happily enough, has the facility to expand to welcome the visitor and in such circumstances can quite easily double its volumetric capacity and become half as long again. It is not always realised, however, how capacious the human vagina can in fact be. There is a case reported by Walter (a matter of fact if we are to believe the Kronohausens' interpretation of "My Secret Life"), in which a

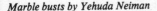

Marble busts by Yehuda Neiman

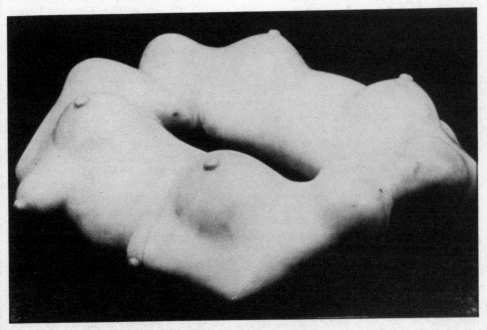

woman is encouraged to insert as many coins as possible into her vagina. Walter produced five English pounds – "all in shillings" – and attempted to insert as many coins as possible into the woman's capacious tract. "Shilling after shilling I put up her, until forty were embedded in the elastic gully . . ." On and on she went until no less than seventy coins were inserted – "Triumphantly, she walked up and down the room, none falling out of her vagina." In the event the woman, Nellie, managed to retain eighty-four shillings in this manner – "I wish someone would do this every day."

Most remarkable tricks played by vagina

The vagina, usually associated with sexual intercourse and childbirth, can be employed in a variety of other ways. In addition to serving as a money-box the vagina can also play the part of a billiard table, a game seemingly favoured in parts of Scandinavia. Thus one writer (J. C. Lauret in "The Danish Sex Fairs") remarks "The ladies will lift up their skirts . . . They will sit against the wall, their legs spread well apart. The gentlemen will take their places on the opposite side of the room . . . Everyone has a try. The object is to flick the glass marbles into the hole of this delightful billiard table. One can guess at the winner's reward . . ." But this is passive on the part of the woman. The vagina has other possibilities. It can, for instance, drink a glass of whisky or play a mouth organ notices E. Chou in "The Dragon and the Phoenix".

Most remarkable vaginal contents

Medical men have been called upon to extract a wide variety of objects from the vagina and urethra following masturbation or accident. Usually the woman knew that the object was inside her and requested medical assistance. Sometimes however a foreign body can lodge in the vagina, after an accident of some sort, and the woman can be totally unaware of its presence. A remarkable instance of this sort occurred when a woman fell downstairs (D. W. T. Roberts' "Clinical Surgery", Vol. 15). A broken-off handle of a broom entered the vagina through the buttock. This was not noticed by her or by the casualty officer who treated her. The broom handle remained undetected in the woman's vagina for three months. Eventually the vaginal discharge made her visit her own practitioner, whereupon the offending object was detected and removed.

First vaginal transplant

A woman aged twenty-one in Salonica was reported as having a boyfriend, two years after receiving a vagina transplant from her mother aged fifty. A professor at the city's university was reported as saying there had been no signs of tissue rejection. The woman's previous deformity had led to the dissolution of her first marriage. The operation to equip her with a new genital tract was apparently successful ("Guardian", 5/3/73).

Longest human clitoris

Clitoris size has only rarely been of importance in human society. A few communities – Ford and Beach mention the Easter Islanders – have favoured the large clitoris and some natives have tried with varying degrees of success to enlarge this organ in their girls. For the most part, however, with a prevailing indifference in the nineteenth-century and early part of the twentieth-century to sexual arousal in women, the clitoris has been neglected. Needless to say, it varies in size. How big are the largest? Theo Lang in "The Difference Between a Man and a Woman" mentions one recorded instance of a woman having a clitoris 2 in. long, and 3 in. "when fully erect". Pomeroy has remarked that clitorises measuring more than 1 in. are very rare in whites, but may occur in 2 or 3 per cent of blacks – "measurements of 3 in. and more were obtained from perhaps one out of 300 or 400 black women". Benjamin and Masters note in "The Prostitute in Society" that Parent-Duchalet came across a clitoris that measured 3.14 in. The eighteenth-century Swiss biologist, Albrecht von Haller, is said to have come across a woman with a monstrous clitoris no less than 7 in. long. But the record clitoris is almost certainly the 12 in. specimen mentioned by various writers and quoted (without comment) by W. Francis Benedict in "The Sexual Anatomy of Women".

BATTERY OPERATED BOTTOM PINCHER

MADE IN ITALY

Largest buttocks

The largest buttocks occur in cases of steatopygy, generally associated with Hottentot, Bushman, and other African tribes. The condition is said to be rare in white women. In its most developed state each buttock can be two or three feet across; and even the youngest members of the tribe can exhibit enormously inflated posteriors. Montegazza has included a number of pictures of women with posterior steatopygy.

Longest female pubic hair

Pubic hair, short and curly in most of us, sometimes grows to quite extraordinary lengths. Havelock Ellis worked as a midwife in his early days, and he notes that only in one case did long pubic hair hamper his efforts. In some remarkable cases recorded by a certain Mr. F. L. John (1778–1852) the pubic hair was longer than the women's ordinary hair. Thus (Paulini): the pubic hair reached the knees. . . . (Bartholia): the pubic hair was plaited behind the woman's back. Ronald Learsall, who nicely notes these instances, observes with appropriate insight that such cases "are unquestionably freakish."

Most prolific growth of pubic hair

There is long pubic hair and there is pubic hair that is thick and expansive in the general abdominal area. Walter (of "My Secret Life"), an evident connoisseur in such matters, talks with clear delight of a fine bush of "Scots red" pubic hair – "The bush was long and thick, twisting and curling in masses half-way up to her navel, and it spread about 5 in. up her buttocks, gradually getting shorter there." In another part of his autobiography Walter remarks that he has seen those "bare of hair, those with but hairy stubble, those with bushes six inches long, covering them from bum bone to navel." And he adds reflectively – "there is not much that I have not seen, felt or tried, with respect to this supreme female article." In like vein, in the "Memoires of Dolly Morton", an American classic, the attributes of Miss Dean are noted with some surprise (she is stripped and beaten for helping runaway slaves) – her spot was covered with a "thick forest of glossy dark brown hair," with locks nearly two inches long. One man remarked, "But Gosh! I've never seen such a fleece between a woman's legs in my life. Darn me if she wouldn't have to be sheared before man could get into her."

From "Every Woman's Book" by Carlile, an early, unusually normal depiction of pubic hair.

Earliest growth of male pubic hair

Pubic hair, normally a sign of the onset of puberty, can occur – as can menstruation – at a surprisingly early age. H. Jolly mentions a boy of only eighteen months who had both an enlarged penis and pubic hair. Often such conditions are associated with a number of other abnormalities. In the cited case the boy "presented with a right-sided abdominal mass." Autopsy showed the mass to be a primary hepatoblastoma.

Latest growth of female pubic hair

In some women there is little pubic hair growth at any time. Such a circumstance can occur in women sexually normal in every other respect. In yet other women **16** pubic hair may eventually grow in a com-

pletely normal way but may commence growth at a surprisingly early or late age. In the Kinsey survey some women did not have any pubic hair until they reached the age of eighteen. It is unlikely that this is a record. We may reasonably speculate that some women in their early twenties have not yet started to grow hair in the genital area.

Earliest growth of female pubic hair

In the "normality spread," as shown, for example, in Kinsey (p.123) some girls began growing pubic hair as early as eight years of age. This is very young to begin such growth yet cannot be considered "abnormal." The real records relate to instances of sexual precocity often, as we

RESTAWHILE
OLD
FOLKS'
HOME
-
RULES:

"I don't know about you, but I'm pinning all my hopes on being a late developer!"

have seen, connected with (sometimes fatal) abnormalities. Hugh Jolly noted instances of pubic hair in babies, in one case a girl of only one month old had hair growth around the genitals.

Latest onset of male potency
We have noted that unusual boys may ejaculate as early as eight years of age. As we may expect, there are surprisingly late upper extremes as well. There are of course sad cases of life-long ejaculatory impotence. But assuming that most men start ejaculating at some time in their lives what is the latest age for such a commencement? According to Kinsey the latest ages of first ejaculation reliably recorded "are 21 for two apparently healthy males, 24 for a religiously inhibited individual, and 22 and 24 for two males with hormonal deficiencies."

Youngest sexually potent male
The earliest ejaculation remembered by any of the "apparently normal males" surveyed by Kinsey was at the age of eight: this age was noted by three males. The

history was also taken of one unusual boy, a Negro interviewed when he was 12, who reckoned he first ejaculated at the age of six. A clinician had diagnosed the boy as "idiopathically precocious in development." In the literature – Kinsey quotes three cases – there are clinical instances of still younger ages. Non-motile sperm have been detected in urine after prostate massage at four and half years. Kinsey opts for eight as the earliest reliably recorded ejaculation.

Oldest woman to menstruate
The onset and termination of menstruation is subject, like all other sexual phenomena, to immense variation. It has been known for a girl to start menstruating at three months old (H. Jolly in "Sexual Precocity", Proc. Royal Soc. Med. 44, 1951), and occasionally the menopause too occurs at a very early age: there are instances of girls reaching the menopause before the age of twenty. The menopause rarely occurs after the age of fifty-five but rare cases do occur. In one instance menstruation was continuing in a woman aged 104.

17

Latest to menstruate

Menstruation, commonly functioning in the vast bulk of teenage girls, may be delayed well past the teens. In a number of cases medical attention needs to be sought; in others the condition may exist in a "normal" but "slow" girl. In the Kinsey sample some girls did not start menstruating until they were in their twenties. The latest instance was a girl who started to menstruate when she was twenty-five years old.

Most famous nymphomaniac in antiquity

Valeria Messalina of ancient Rome almost certainly wins this one; indeed her name (the "Messalina complex") has been used as a synonym for nymphomania. With her insatiable sexual appetites she acted as

Messalina, Roman Empress of Claudius, the most famous of all nymphomaniacs.

prostitute and seducer. She married Claudius when only sixteen; it has been speculated that she started an active sex life when she was thirteen or fourteen. If she fancied a man, Claudius would order him to submit to her whims: it was useful being married to an emperor. Dio Cassius has declared that she kept her lustful husband well supplied with housemaids for bedfellows. She often enjoyed herself in the local brothel.

Most frequent physiological cause of nymphomania

In their book "Nymphomania", Albert Ellis and Edward Sagarin represent the failure in a woman – through *physiological* rather than *psychological* reasons – to achieve orgasm as the "most frequent *physiological* cause of nymphomania" (p. 95). This is a highly contentious subject. Not much work has been done on it, and it is extremely difficult to say what is a *physiological,* and what a *psychological,* block to experience of orgasm.

Most frequent psychological cause of nymphomania

According to Ellis and Sargarin, *one outstanding reason* why a woman becomes a nymphomaniac in our society is through "an overwhelming need to be loved, a hunger that generally seems to be greater in women, than in men." Thus – in her efforts to seek out affection, security, and acceptance – she comes to have many sexual experiences that she might otherwise not welcome. There is a clear sense in which this is a patriarchal interpretation of female sexuality. Not all male writers are ready to come to the conclusion that a fair number of women can simply enjoy sex and see it as worth experiencing for its own sake.

Best non-medical description of a hermaphrodite

The medical literature abounds with descriptions of the various types of hermaphroditism. Sometimes a good *non-medical* description is produced. Perhaps the best is that in Henry Spender Ashbee's "Catena Librorum Tacendorum". The "woman" was fairly attractive. Ashbee said – "She was about twenty years of age, rather pretty, and quite womanly, with beautiful eyes, a good complexion, and fair hair; her nose was rather masculine and her mouth rather rough and large, with bad teeth; her chest was expansive, and her breasts well developed; the lower part of the legs slightly bowed, and masculine. She possessed, in appearance at least, the organs of both sexes, but neither perfect, a small penis, as in a lad of twelve or fourteen years, and testicles apparently developed; the yard was, however, not perforated. Underneath the testicles was what seemed to be a perfect female vestibule, of which the opening was, however, only large enough to allow her to pass water, but not to receive a man, or even to admit the insertion of the end of a quill ... she had no monthly flow, but felt, nevertheless, a periodic indisposition; she experienced pleasures in the embraces of both sexes, and had even an erection when with a sympathetic female. She could not, of course, satisfy her desires."

Rarest type of human hermaphrodites

The rarest cases of human hermaphroditism are the instances of *true* or *gonadal hermaphrodite*. In this condition each gonad is an ovotestis – part ovary and part testis – or one is an ovary and the other a testis. Swyer, writing in 1954, remarks that only forty cases had been recorded in all the medical literature. The condition can be diagnosed only by microscopial examination of parts of the gonads.

Among the outward signs in a "male" are hypospadias, undescended testicles and abnormal breast development; in the "female" with this condition there is abnormal development of the clitoris. Normal spermato-genesis may occur close to an ovary in which ovulation takes place.

Most famous sex-change Court case

The most famous "sex-change" case to get to court was that of England's April Ashley. She had been born with male genitals but was psychologically female, i.e. she was a transsexual. She hated her penis and in 1960 underwent an operation to remove the visible signs of maleness: strictly speaking this was not a change of sex, since all she had accomplished was to remove the visible evidence of her genetic sex. In the eyes of the law she was still a man (and in fact had been brought up as George Jamieson). In February 1970 her marriage to Arthur Corbett was declared null on the ground that she was not really married. Mr. Justice Ormrod declared that

"She is a biological male and has been so since birth." She had male chromosomes and male gonads. Lawyers supported the court ruling but medical opinion was divided. Dr. Benjamin, author of "The Transsexual Phenomenon", noted that "April Ashley has a vagina, so she is a woman." For April Ashley herself the court ruling was a personal disaster.

Most thoroughly investigated virgin birth

There have been many claims of virgin birth in human history, strong in legend (Greek mythology, the Bible etc.) and weak in the medical literature. In some rare cases a woman has carried part of her twin around inside her and subsequent "delivery" has created the illusion of virgin birth. In November 1955 the "London Sunday Pictorial" asked women to come forward who thought that there had been no father to their child. Nineteen claims were made to the newspaper and these were investigated. Eleven were negated in the initial enquiry because the mothers thought an intact hymen inevitably indicated a virgin conception. Finally the nineteen cases were reduced to one possible. Mrs. E. Jones and her daughter were subjected to further thorough investigation. Their blood, saliva and tasting powers were all examined, and attempts were made to graft skin from one to the other. Blood, saliva, and tasting powers were almost identical, but the grafts did not take. In June 1956 the Sunday Pictorial was prepared to state that, after six months of detailed medical investigation, the results were consistent with a case of virgin birth. Professor J. B. S. Haldane disagreed and argued that the evidence in fact led to the opposite conclusion – the child had a father.

First discovery of sperm

Human sperm were first discovered by a student of Antonij van Leeuwenhoek in 1677 in the city of Delft. The name of the student is not known for certain: he is variously written up as Ludwig Hamm, van Hamm or von Hammen. According to some writers he is a Dutchman, to others a German. One day he brought to the acknowledged master of microscopy, Leeuwenhoek, a bottle containing semen

A student of Leeuwenhoek (below, with his microscope) is credited with the first discovery of sperm. Right up to the end of 17th c., male spermatozoa was surrounded by mystery. Right, as it was understood by Uartsoeher (1655-1725).

and pointed out that small animals could be seen moving about in the ejaculate. Van Leeuwenhoek went on to study the seminal emissions from a wide range of sick and healthy men; in the semen of them all the odd creatures could be detected. He described his findings to the Royal Society in London –

I have seen so excessively great a quantity of living animalcules that I am much astonished by it. I can say without exaggeration that in a bit of matter no longer than a grain of sand more than fifty thousand animalcules were present, whose shape I can compare with nought better than with our river eel. These animalcules move about with uncommon vigour and in some places clustered so thickly together that they formed a single dark mass. After a short time they separated. In fine, these animals astonished my eye more than aught I had seen before.

Of course at the end of the seventeenth-century there was still a mystery as to what sperm actually were. Some thought them to be parasites in the seminal fluid – and saliva and urine and other bodily secretions were quickly examined in the search for more sperm. Others thought them coagulating agents.

First discovery of sperm as fertilizing agent

It was not realized that sperm were concerned in the process of fertilization until the nineteenth century. Various names are associated with the discovery – Prevost and Dumas (1824), Peltier (1835), and Dujardin (1837).

First sperm bank

The idea of an effective sperm bank has appealed to eugenically-minded individuals for a good few centuries. Such arrangements have only recently become practically feasible. The first two sperm banks, set up in Iowa City and Tokyo, both began life in 1964.

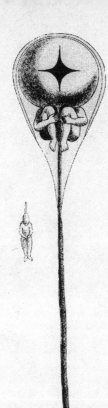

First sperm-bank child
The first sperm-bank child was born in the U.S. in 1953 – and, in the words of Gerald Leach, was "perfectly normal". Since then the numbers have swelled, with the sperm storage period being gradually lengthened. It seems that little ecological or eugenic thought has gone into this subject.

Most famous victims of VD
A great number of famous and talented men have had one sort of venereal illness or another. Here are one or two of them – Abraham, David and Job, Caesar, Herod, Tiberius, Charlemagne, Charles V and VIII of France, John of Gaunt, Popes Alexander VI, Julius II and Leo X, Henry VIII, Erasmus, Albrecht Durer, Thomas Wolsey, Ivan the Terrible, Benvenuto Cellini, Richelieu, John Aubrey, Casanova, Boswell, Goethe, Schopenhauer, Keats, Schubert, Nietzsche, Mussolini, Hitler, Gauguin, Strindberg, Oscar Wilde, etc., etc. (See T. Rosebury, "Microbes and Morals"). This list could easily be extended.

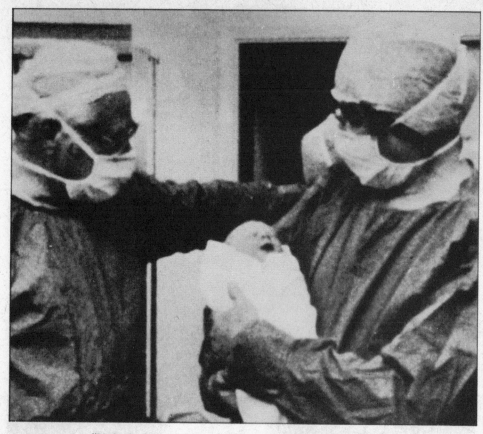

"Medical childbirth" — the first test-tube baby, Louise Brown

Most extreme reaction to contact with semen

Most women don't mind semen too much, though some unduly fastidious ones complain about its smell or stickiness. Some females, however, have a quite extraordinary reaction to seminal fluid: they are happily rare. In one case reported in 1967 a girl had an acute allergic reaction to human sperm. She came from a family with a long history of various kinds of allergy, including eczema, asthma, and dermatitis. A short time after her first sexual experience she developed a rash and asthma; her lips, eyelids, tongue, and throat became swollen, she had violent pains in the pelvis and finally lost consciousness. Most of these symptoms appeared every time she had sexual intercourse: they began within half an hour and lasted well into the next day. When semen diluted one part per million was injected under her skin it left an angry weal, so intense was the girl's reaction (P. Vaughan "The Pill on Trial").

Most powerful attributes accorded to semen

Most of us know that semen has the remarkable ability to help start babies. But this is only one of the powers attributed to the mysterious substance. One idea is that semen has a "magnetic" effect those who retain their semen i.e. refrain from sexual activity, are able to draw both men and women to themselves. It has often been assumed that semen has mystical or religious powers. Thus a subsect of the Gnostics mixed the fluid with the sacramental draught in their religious ceremonies. And in the so-called Black Mass, semen has served as holy water. Aleister Crowley reckoned that art, literature and philosophy were all the outcome of sexual power, and that the whole of human psychology was a radiating miasma from the seminal stream: he is reported as saying that "Mind is a disease of semen."

22

Right: Aleister Crowley, "the Beast"

Part II

Sexual Technique
&
Performance

Oldest aphrodisiac

Some aphrodisiacs have been popular since the days of antiquity. The mandrake plant is mentioned in the Old Testament and is still in use today. Mandrake (or madragora, mandragora officinarum) is a member of the potato family with a large dark-brown root and small red fruit. It contains the alkaloids atropine and scopolomine: in mild doses these are soporifics; in larger doses they can kill! In antiquity there were magical rules for harvesting the plant. Pliny noted that the plant roots were in the form of human genitals – which explains, through the idea of sympathetic magic, the supposed aphrodisiac effect. Cantharides, another ancient aphrodisiac, was first mentioned by Aristotle: its active principle, cantharidin, is extracted from the dried and powdered bodies of the blister beetle, a brown or bluish creature found in southern Europe. Yet another old alleged aphrodisiac is ginseng, the "mystic plant of the Orient", made into tablets by modern sex aid retailers and also into a wine. In the Far East today ginseng wine is termed kaoling (as strong as vodka), with the roots of ginseng soaked in the cask for at least three years. Users are recommended to take a small glass before going to bed.

Most bizarre aphrodisiac

An endless range of bizarre concoctions have been devised with the aim of restoring failing sexual powers. Sometimes, as we have seen, plants were used because of their physical resemblance to the human genital organs. Drugs have always been popular. Perhaps the most bizarre types of aphrodisiac are those involving an element of cannibalism. We all know of the use of parts of non-human animals to increase human potency (a Chinese Emperor, for example, kept a herd of deer so he could drink their blood to increase his virile powers); but often it was thought desirable also to consume parts of men and women for this purpose. Menstrual blood, placenta, and genitals have all been devoured to increase sexual prowess; semen was also popular. ("The semen of virile young men should be mixed with the excrement of hawks or eagles and taken in pellet form.") Chinese eunuchs, seeking regeneration of their lost sexual organs, would hopefully eat the warm brains of newly decapitated criminals.

Most famous Oriental aphrodisiac

Despite the legendary nature of ginseng most of us in the West are more likely to have heard of the various uses to which opium has been put. This drug has in fact been employed optimistically as an aphrodisiac over the centuries. Even a mild dose of opium is supposed by Orientals to provide about one hour of continuous genital stimulation – "assuring the desideratum of at least three thousand phallic thrusts"; it is worth quoting further the poetic mention of the opium pill as it appears in Chin P'ing Mei –

> Take but a speck of this,
>   set it upon you, then
> Rush like a whirlwind
>   to the bridal chamber
> The first engagement
>   will leave you full of vigour;
> The second, even stronger than before.
> Though twelve exquisite beauties,
>   all arrayed in scarlet, wait your onset,
> You may enjoy each one,
>   according to your fancy . . .
> And so on and so forth – "Ten women
>   in one night will be as one to you."

Most detailed Chinese aphrodisiac recipe

There are some immensely complicated formulae for ancient Chinese aphrodisiacs. A number of these, from the Wang Tao "Collection of Secret Prescriptions", are quoted by Eric Chou. One example will suffice here (for use in the spring) 1 fen = 0.36 grams –

Fuling (underground fungus)	– 4 fen
Ch'ang p'u (Acorus calamus)	– 4 fen
Shan chu yu (plant)	– 4 fen
K'u lou root (herb)	– 4 fen
T'u ssu tzu (herb seeds)	– 4 fen
Niu ch'i (herb)	– 4 fen
Dry ti huang (Rebmannia)	– 7 fen
Hsi hsin (wild ginger)	– 4 fen
Fan feng (herb)	– 4 fen
Shu yu (yam root)	– 4 fen
Hsu tuan (herb)	– 4 fen

The ingredients of this prescription, as with other concoctions were to be ground down and made into pills.

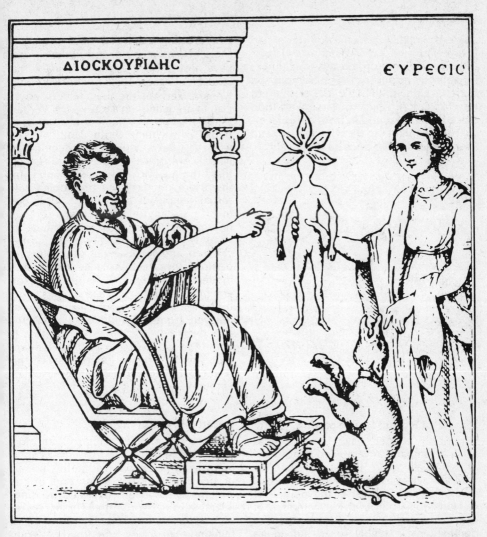

ΔΙΟCΚΟΥΡΙΔΗC

ΕΥΡΕCΙC

Dioscrides being handed a mandrake uprooted by a dog, which dies in the process.

Most complicated frigidity cure

As we have seen, some of the most complex remedies for lack of sexual capacity and interest are the various forms of aphrodisiac concoction. Perhaps equally complex are the rules governing collection of plant or animal ingredients. As a cure for frigidity it was often thought necessary not only to mix a complex of herbs and animal parts together – often cemented into pills by means of honey – but also to perform a number of ritualistic moves over the compound. Magic was often thought to aid chemistry. In one cure for frigidity it was thought necessary to search out a particular species of red bat which rested in pairs amid the red flowers of banana trees. The bats were dried, ground into powder, and hopefully spread on a woman externally to make her feel sexy.

Most bizarre love-charm

In ancient Irish legend amorous girls were said to invade graveyards in the search of corpses buried nine days. When they found one they cut from the body a narrow strip of skin extending from the top of the head down to the extremity of one foot. They then tried to knot the length of dead skin round the arm or leg of a sleeping lover and to remove it before he awoke. If the girl kept the skin hidden from all eyes, and managed to perform her 27 task every night – so long would the man love her! Canidia, the Witch of Horace's fifth "Epode", got up to even worse tricks for aphrodisiac purposes. For example, she buried a kidnapped boy in the earth up to his chin and left him to starve with food placed on the ground in front of his face – so that she might use his bone marrow and liver in love potions once he was dead.

Highest estimate of female passion

Historically women have been seen as sexually rampant, as vamp and temptress – or as sexually dead (the proper state for "moral" wives). One index of sexual awareness and interest is the degree of masturbation in an individual (though of course masturbation may be infrequent or non-existent in highly sexed individuals when an adequacy of other outlets exists). Masturbation is said to be so widespread among both married and unmarried Muslim females throughout Africa and the East that "it is commonly regarded by the menfolk as customary and matter-of-fact" (A. Edwards & R. E. L. Masters, "The Cradle of Erotica"). "Rubbing" or "pounding" is considered a natural manifestation of feminine nature – for "women's passion is ten times greater than man's." In this spirit it has been suggested that since it takes ten men to satisfy one women, it is only normal that a woman faithful to one man should masturbate from time to time to satisfy sexual needs. (French troops marching off to war were said to provide their wives with dildos to reduce the chances of adultery in their absence.)

Lowest estimate of female passion

Moralists and men nervous of their virility have always been eager to suggest that sexual feelings are weak or non-existent in women. Perhaps the most famous physician to argue in such a way was Sir William Acton who wrote a number of sexological books in the nineteenth century – and who has been roundly condemned by liberals ever since. He wrote, for instance, that "the majority of women (happily for them) are not very much troubled with sexual feeling of any kind ... The best mothers, wives, and managers of households, know little or nothing of sexual indulgence. Love of home, children, and domestic duties, are the only passions they feel. As a general rule, a modest woman seldom desires any sexual gratification for herself. She submits to her husband, but ... would far rather be relieved from his attentions ..." Acton also declared, in stronger terms, that to impute sexual feeling to a woman is a "vile aspersion," though he conceded that women of the lower classes may have such emotions.

Lowest estimate of frigidity

Acton presumably thought that most women were frigid, and that such a condition was to be encouraged in the interest of propriety. At the other end of the extreme it has been suggested by many liberal sexologists that there is in fact no such thing as a frigid women, that women thinking themselves to be frigid either do not have a sexual partner whom they love or have been given wrong information about the nature of orgasm. Thus the Hegelers (in "An ABZ of Love") state that "In all the cases in which contended frigidity has been carefully examined it has been found that the woman in question certainly did have sexual feelings".

Most sexually inhibited species

Man, proud of his imagined superiority over the rest of the animal kingdom, can hardly be rated a winner in the sexual stakes. His sexual organs are neither the largest nor the most impressive performers; his copulatory capacities are outstripped by many animal species; and he is hardly the most prolific reproductively. In

addition man is much more likely to get sexual hang-ups than any other animal. If a snake fancies a bit of necrophilia, a marten a bit of rape, or a porpoise a bit of group sex, then such individuals are unlikely to experience inhibiting feelings of guilt at the thought. Man, however, is beset by anxiety, fear, guilt and moral loathing with regard to many fancied sexual activities: few individuals indeed have come to terms with their sexuality. With all his psychosexual problems man is without doubt the most sexually inhibited among animal species.

Most extreme consequences of orgasm

Orgasm, stressing the body in various ways, has been known to produce some dire consequences. Kinsey again – "At orgasm some individuals may remain unconscious for a matter of seconds or even for some minutes". Kinsey also notes more than a dozen authorities – from Roubaud (1876) to Brown and Kempton (1950) – who recorded "loss of sensory capacity or even of consciousness during extreme emotion or sexual arousal". And orgasm has been known to accompany a variety of forms of damage to the body – including lesions and ruptures of various organs. Death has also occurred from time to time!

Latest to respond to orgasm

Kinsey also went to some lengths to ascertain the "age at first response to orgasm." We have already indicated the youngest orgasms for both girls and boys. At the other extreme there are many women who reached the age of late forties without experiencing orgasm. In particular, Kinsey notes three women who had not reached their first orgasm until they were between forty-eight and fifty years of age. It should be stressed however that lack of orgasm is not synonymous with lack of sexual response, and that a very satisfying sex-life can coexist with lack of orgasm.

Most common types of male orgasm

Kinsey delineated six types of male orgasm. In part the types vary according to the intensity of the reaction exhibited. The most common type of male orgasm – supposedly characterising about 45 per cent of adult males – features some body tension. There may also be twitching or tension in one or both legs, of the mouth, of the arms, or of other particular parts of the body. There is gradual build-up to a climax which involves rigidity of the whole body and a degree of throbbing in the penis. There is orgasm with a few spasms but little after-effect. This is seen as the 29 most common type of male orgasm (discussed in I. Singer "The Goals of Human Sexuality").

Fastest achieved male orgasm

It is interesting to note how quickly the "preadolescent" can respond to sexual stimulation. Kinsey tabulated the percentage of the population who could respond to the point of orgasm in less than ten seconds of sexual stimulation. No less than 6.4 per cent of preadolescents could achieve orgasm in less than ten seconds of sexual stimulation. And a quarter of all those tested could manage orgasm in less than one minute. Kinsey notes that erection is much quicker in preadolescent boys than in adults; and some two-year-olds come to climax in less than ten seconds.

Most frequent male orgasm

Frequency of orgasm has, like most other male sexual parameters, often been taken as defining sexual worth. The more orgasms the better, has been a general cry. It would not help the ego of most men to learn they can generally be beaten in this area by young boys. In the Kinsey data, in a series of 182 observed cases, 81 of the preadolescent boys achieved orgasm only once. 17 achieved it twice, 42 achieved it three, four or five times in succession, 30 achieved it from six to ten times in succession and 12 achieved it more than ten times in succession. The undisputed record was twenty-one orgasms in a row. One eleven-month-old baby boy managed fourteen orgasms in thirty-eight minutes; one eleven-year-old had eleven orgasms in an hour; a fourteen-year-old had eleven orgasms in four hours, and so on and so forth. It should be remembered that such startling multiorgasmic capabilities are generally lost at the time when orgasm is accompanied by the ejaculation of semen. At the same time there are some adult men who achieve high orgasmic performance over a long period. Kinsey records the case of one man who had three orgasms a day over a period of thirty years, and one who averaged 33.1 orgasms a week over a thirty-year period.

Fastest achieved female orgasm

We are all led to believe that women are slower to achieve orgasm than are men. This is a more complicated picture than it seems – not least because, as some have

argued, coitus itself may not be the most effective way to arouse a woman. Be this as it may it is still true that many women respond very quickly to sexual stimulation. Fisher notes that in one series of surveys the average woman seemed to require about 8 minutes to achieve orgasm – "but it should be emphasised that there was a remarkable individual variation, with some women requiring as little as 1 minute and others requiring as much as 30 minutes to reach orgasm." If, in a relatively small research survey, women were found who could achieve orgasm in less than 1 minute it is reasonable to surmise that some would require only 40 or 50 seconds to achieve the same result. And doubtless there are some "freakish" folk requiring much less time than this; for instance, the women noted by Pomeroy who achieved orgasm 2-5 seconds after penile insertion!

Slowest to achieve female orgasm

In the Fisher study some women required as much as 30 minutes stimulation to achieve orgasm. This is a relatively long

time but perhaps such women are consoled at the thought that some of their sexually active sisters never have orgasm at all and are perfectly happy. As we have suggested before, it is a mistake to think that a sexually satisfactory life needs to be punctuated at regular intervals by well-defined orgasms. The tardy orgasm may or may not cause distress, but it should always be stressed that there is more to sex than orgasm.

Longest female orgasms

The idea of orgasm as climax suggests that it is soon over, and this is indeed true. At the same time a single orgasm can sometimes roll on and on with the man – or more likely the woman – carried along on waves of bliss. According to Fisher the typical female orgasm lasts from 6 to 10 seconds. In a few extreme cases in the various samples, it was reported that orgasm lasts "more than 20 seconds". With the general spread of human ability we may expect a record orgasm to last for around half a minute!

Most frequent female orgasms
If the feminists want evidence of female superiority to men in the sexual sphere they should look to female multiorgasmic capabilities. In a "Playboy" interview with Timothy Leary we learn of the effects of LSD on a woman's orgasmic capacities –

> Playboy: We've heard that some women who ordinarily have difficulty achieving orgasm find themselves capable of multiple orgasms under LSD. Is that true?
> Leary: In a carefully prepared, loving LSD session, a woman can have several hundred orgasms.
> Playboy: Several *hundred?*
> Leary: Yes. Several hundred.

That female orgasms can be reckoned in hundreds – in the most extreme cases – in a single session may seem absurd. There is a body of evidence however to suggest that such a possibility could obtain in fact, Brecher, for instance, quotes the experience of a male participant in the Sexual Freedom Movement – "I would estimate that she experienced between 100 and 200 orgasms during the 4 hour period. Her orgasms were quite obviously

physiological; there was no possibility of 'pretending'." Pomeroy notes "one woman who was capable of from fifteen to twenty orgasms in twenty minutes". Cauthery and Cole declare that "the world's standing record is 100 in one hour," though they give no reference for this remarkable accomplishment.

Least sensitive erogenous zone
Many men are keen to play with a woman's vulva: women are often relatively indifferent to such activity – particularly if the man focuses on the outer lips. The inside lips (labia minora) are usually highly sensitive, the outer lips (labia majora) much less so. The women surveyed by Fisher rated the sexual excitement areas in the following sequence – clitoris, vagina, near clitoris, inside lips of vulva, inside vagina, and breasts. The outside lips of the vulva were rated the least excitable of all.

Rarest orgasmic technique
Various extremely unusual masturbatory techniques have been used by both men

and women to achieve orgasm, and, with men ejaculation. It is a commonplace that fantasy accompanied by digital manipulation of the penis, can produce ejaculation in the majority of men. A small number, however, can accomplish ejaculation by means of fantasy alone. In the Kinsey survey of more than 5000 men, three or four were found who could ejaculate by deliberately concentrating on sexual fantasies, without any genital manipulation – "In such a case the psychic stimulation is entirely responsible for the result." Two or three males in a thousand are able to suck their own penises to achieve orgasm and ejaculation.

Least frequent dreams without orgasm
The least frequent sexual dreams without orgasm are much the same whether the dreamer has "overt experience" or not. In the Kinsey survey two types of dreams without orgasm were experienced by only two per cent of people: these were dreams of sexual contact with animals and dreams having a clear sado-masochistic content. Dreams of rape were noted by four per cent of the women surveyed.

Most frequent dreams with orgasm
In general fewer people report dreams with orgasm than dreams without orgasm. Orgasmic dreams, in people without "overt experience," were most frequently connected with coitus in the Kinsey female survey – though here only 10 per cent of women reported orgasmic dreams of coitus. The next most frequent type of dream – reported by seven per cent of women – was homosexual in character. Thirty-nine per cent of women "with experience prior to interview" reported orgasmic dreams of coitus – and the same percentage also noted orgasmic dreams in a non-coital heterosexual situation.

Least frequent dreams with orgasm
Dreams of petting and dreams having sado-masochistic content were less frequently reported, as an orgasmic experience in those women without "overt experience," than any other category of sexual dreams. In fact both those types of dreams were reported by only one per

cent of the women in the Kinsey survey. Dreams of pregnancy and childbirth were accompanied by orgasm in two per cent of the "inexperienced" women surveyed. Dreams of contact with animals produced orgasms in twice this number of women – in four per cent of those surveyed. In "experienced" women the least frequent types of dreams producing orgasm were those connected with animal contacts, dreams having sado-masochistic content, and dreams relating to pregnancy or childbirth. All these types of dreams produced orgasms in one per cent of women surveyed.

Maximum pulse rate in coitus
Graphic analogies have been drawn between human coitus and other forms of energetic activity, such as riding a bicycle or running a sprint. In all such cases various physiological effects can be noted, one of which is the more rapid circulation of blood. In the 1950's Kinsey pointed out that "precise measurements on the increase in pulse rate during arousal are few," a circumstance which – to a degree – Masters and Johnson have rectified. Mendelsohn produced graphs showing maximum pulse rate for men and women before, during and after coitus: a maximum pulse rate of 150 was recorded. Boas and Goldschmidt recorded maximums of 146 in four consecutive orgasms in a woman. And Klumbies and Kleinsorge noted a maximum pulse rate of 142 in a man at orgasm. In violent exercise boys have been known to reach a rate of 200; and young men running to a treadmill have reached 208.

Oldest potent couple
All relevant surveys have shown men and women still having sexual intercourse when in their eighties or even nineties, though around three-quarters of all men are impotent by the time they reach their eighties. The oldest potent male in the Kinsey survey was an 88-year-old Negro, who continued to enjoy regular sexual intercourse with his ninety-year-old wife! It should be said that some cases of impotence in old men are certainly due to the absence of adequate stimulation: though it is arguable that sudden stimula- **33**

The lovers are having sexual intercourse, an episode that illustrates the kind of steady nerve on which the 18th century Rajput military castes prided themselves.

tion to orgasm in an old man could prove fatal as has happened.

Longest sustained intercourse

The act of putting the penis inside the vagina but deliberately holding back from orgasm has been termed coitus reservatus. It has also been denoted Karezza in Sanskrit and Hindu literature. In some instances it has been practised by whole communities, as in the Oneida Colony in the nineteenth century in New York State. The "colony" founded by Noyes in Vermont in 1841, moved to Oneida in 1848. What Noyes called "male continence" meant the man putting his penis inside the woman's vagina for periods of well over an hour and then withdrawing, without ejaculation, after the woman had experienced several orgasms. The practice has been known throughout the world. It has been pointed out that busy men in China, "in the habit of spending hours each day" with concubines, would still manage to see to their affairs – "There are many instances in both novels and court records, of papers being signed without the male member being withdrawn, and of urgent matters being discussed with callers to the accompaniment of occasional

movements to ensure that the erection was not lost." Mohammed was said to have recommended prolonged coitus of this type.

Most frequent sexual activity

We have already noted the most frequent orgasms for men and women. Obviously orgasmic frequency is related to coitus but only partly: there are other ways in which a person can come to climax. Kinsey found that some married couples were having sexual intercourse as many as twenty-nine times a week, i.e. couples in the 21-25 year age group. By the age of fifty, "maximum frequency" had dropped to around 14 times a week. And it has also been noted that in some exceptional cases, from the youngest lovers to those around forty years of age – "there were some individuals who were having coitus in their marriages on an average of four times a day, every day in the week. By the age of fifty-five no couples in the Kinsey sample were having coitus more frequently than seven or eight times a week. During one family planning trial in Britain one woman logged on her specially provided record that she had intercourse ninety-one times in one month – "a figure considered so

extraordinary that it was left out of the final calculation in case it ruined the figures for average frequency of copulation (about once every fourth day)". In their extensive cross-cultural study, Ford and Beach noted that Thonga males copulate with 3 or 4 wives in a single night; and Chegga men are supposed to have intercourse as many as ten times a night. But does orgasm occur in each copulation – "the data unfortunately permit no definitive statements."

Most active sex life in old age
Kinsey found men still making love about once a week at the age of sixty-five. In one group 75-year-olds were having sex about once a month; and 80-year-olds were managing it once every nine or ten weeks. The record for such things lies with a white man who was having – at the age of seventy – more than seven ejaculations per week!

Most frequent extra-marital sex
In Kinsey we find that extra-marital intercourse is most frequent in the 21-25 years age group i.e. a maximum frequency of about eighteen times a week. Homosexual activity, coitus with prostitutes, petting to climax, marital intercourse are also high for this group. Younger people seemingly do better at masturbation and nocturnal emissions.

Steepest erection angle
The average position of the erect penis, observed for all ages, is very slightly above the horizontal. At the same time there are approximately 15 to 20 per cent of cases where the angle is about 45 degrees above the horizontal. In general the angle of erection is higher for males in their early twenties, and lower in more advanced ages. "Average angles become definitely reduced in males past fifty."

Longest maintained erection
For some purposes it may be desirable to maintain an erection for a long time. It is clear that periods of up to an hour are not uncommon, and that if the penis is in the vagina for this time then maintaining an erection is not difficult for some individuals. Kinsey noted that the length o time over which the erection can be maintained under "continuous erotic arousal' drops from an average of nearly an hour in the late teens and early twenties to seven minutes in men in their late sixties. It i pointed out that under prolonged stimulation "many a teen-age male will maintain a continuous erection for several hours . . ."

Fastest erection
Speed of erection varies enormously from one man to another –and in the same man from one sexual encounter to another. Factors such as alcohol and fatigue are highly relevant, as is the degree of erotic arousal. In a few exceptional males (see Kinsey) the erection of the penis may occur in as little as three seconds.

Least active kissers
Most people take the values and practices of their own society as absolute, those of other cultures as subjective and misguided. For those human beings accustomed to kissing it may seem odd that some peoples do not indulge in any such practice. Most of us have heard that Eskimos rub noses rather than kiss. Fewer of us have heard of the Siriono, mentioned in the anthropological literature: this tribe, living in South America, do not indulge in kissing (nor is breast stimulation a usual part of foreplay). Nor do the Thonga go much on kissing: when they first saw Europeans kissing they remarked – "Look at them – they eat each other's saliva and dirt." This is not so odd as it sounds. There are more germs in the mouth than in the anus!

Longest love-making session
It all depends what you mean by lovemaking. Does it count if you knock off for a sandwich and a drink and then start again? No agreed ground-rules have been established. Anyway one figure that will do for a starter is the fifteen hours recorded by Mae West in her autobiography – a man called "Ted" apparently made love to her for this length of time. He later said that "he was both astounded and pleased at his own abilities."

MAE WEST
Paramount Pictures

37

"In bed he just lies there"

Oldest recorded sex play

There is a rich ancient literature dealing with various aspects of non-coital sex technique. Kinsey cites dozens of references to "non-coital petting techniques." For instance, there are ancient Near Eastern documents dating back to the second millenium B.C.; and in Ezekiel XXIII, 3 it is recorded that as people committed 'whoredoms' in various places, "there were their breasts pressed, and there they bruised the teats of their virginity." There is very little new in the modern sex manuals. We may be new-fangled with invitations to try a variety of sex techniques but the ancients did it all, or nearly all, before us.

Longest human kiss

Kisses between men and women usually last for a few seconds. Kisses lasting minutes are unusual; kisses lasting hours quite remarkable. There is a type of kiss called *"maraichinage"* – after the Maraichins or inhabitants of the district Pays de Mont in the Vendée (Britanny) – which quite literally lasts for hours. In this type of exchange the couple mutually explore and caress the inside of each other's mouths with their tongues "as profoundly as possible." Maraichinage has been recommended as a "real antidote against depopulation."

Most effective sex play techniques

What works with one person does not work with another. What is sexually provocative or exciting is in the eye of the beholder. Having said this we should remark that people also have a great deal in common. It would be surprising if it were otherwise: people are, after all, physically and psychologically similar in a number of ways. This similarity allows us to generalize in particular ways, i.e. in connection with what turns people on. A consensus seems to be emerging that of all sex-play techniques the most sexually stimulating is often oral sex – in which one partner kisses, licks, or "tongue-teases" the genitals of the other. If they lie head-to-toe — the celebrated *soixante-neuf* or 69 position – they can of course do it to each other simultaneously.

Most dangerous sex play techniques

Some tricks that people get up to for sexual enjoyment are quite remarkable. Some bondage and sadistic practices are cruel and hardly to be encouraged: in extreme cases people have been whipped to death, crucified on wooden beams, and burned alive. In such instances it is hard to imagine that the participants, willing or not, are unaware of the extreme hazards they run. Sometimes, however, there can be dangers that people do not realize – as, for example, with a man performing oral sex on a woman (*cunnilingus*). If he blows into the vagina, accidently or on purpose, he is quite likely to kill his loved one – through air embolism! Such an event is not designed to prolong a happy relationship. Death in such circumstances can be remarkably rapid, a matter of seconds. There are some such instances in the medical literature.

Most extreme consequence of coitus

The most extreme consequence for any type of human activity is death: and such an unfortunate event has often occurred through coitus. Death during sexual activity was noted by Pliny A.D. 23-79, Hirschfeld, Van de Velde, Havelock Ellis, etc. It has been suggested that some Oriental copulations have been pursued with the very aim of totally exhausting, or even killing, the woman – the Japanese *gokuraku-ojo* or "sweet death". According to Muhammed, to die in the glorious battle abed with one's belly on top is to die a martyr of love. The Caliph Harun er-Reshid was reckoned a hero because he died of heart failure during sexual intercourse. Christian sages have viewed things differently, seeing death in coitus as a final infamy. Attila the Hun was said to have died fornicating with a blonde.

Most active sex play by age

In data based on single unmarried males Kinsey found that the 21-25 year-old group "petted to climax" more frequently than the other ten age ranges surveyed. Even so their record is hardly impressive – a mere seven times a week. Perhaps we should be surprised that this figure is higher than that for the 16-20 year-old group (4.5 times a week as maximum) – but the younger men are perhaps too busy masturbating (15 times a week compared with twelve for the 21-25 year age group).

Most famous sex play advice to royalty

The Empress Maria Theresa consulted her physician Van Sweiten about her sterility. He thought that if she would only come to orgasm then she would be fertile. With this in mind he remarked – "I am of the opinion that the clitoris of your Most

MARIA THERESIA ROM: IMPERATRIX

Sacred Majesty should be titillated for some length of time before coitus." Whether or not the Empress took the advice we do not know; we do of course know that orgasm has nothing to do with conception. The lady did subsequently bear no less than sixteen children – and perhaps she had an enjoyable sex life.

Most frequently quoted Islamic sexual feats

There are many tales, some purportedly true, in which sturdy heroes achieve staggering coital feats. Islamic folklore is full of such instances of prodigious sexual achievement; and no doubt some of the writers liked to think that the stories were based on fact. Two authorities talk of "fifteen forays" being served or of much "thrashing and slashing" and "poking and stroking" all night long. It is said that to be known as *abū zeqqzeqq* (father of thrusts), one capable of "great strokes of the prickle," is a great honour. The Hindu *dhakēlā* (pusher) is a worthy male performer to whom no woman worth her salt **39** would deny herself. And *abū hhimlāt* (father of assaults) is taken as a fitting name for one of those "hardy cocks" of Upper Egypt, who is equipped to "take on twenty hens one after the other."

Most impressive biblical sexual feats

In the Bible and old Hebrew writings there is much about sex, but one has to learn to delve into euphemism and circumlocution to unravel the true meaning. The Talmudists have written that – . . . we read (1 Kings 1, 15), *And Bathsheba went in unto the king into the chamber.* Rab Judah said in Rab's name: "On that occasion Bathsheba dried herself thirteen times." This has been taken as meaning that Bathsheba and David had sexual intercourse thirteen times in succession – and after each orgasm, according to Mosaic law and custom, Bathsheba was obliged to wash and/or dry her genitals. And the Talmud notes, in reference to 2 Samuel II: 2 ("and it came to pass, in the early evening, that David arose from off his bed"), that "he copulated by day instead of night so that he might be free from desire by night." During the day King David copulated with eighteen wives. He records the consequences –

> "I am tired of my moaning; every night I flood my bed with tears (Heb. *dim ath,* prostatic and-or seminal fluid); I soak my couch with my weeping. My strength is exhausted through my groaning all the day long; my moisture (semen) is dried up like the drought of summer. I am poured out like water; my moisture is evaporated as by the heat of the hot seasong I am weary of my weeping (continual ejaculations)."

Most impressive sexual performance by race

In their cross-cultural study of sexual performance Dord and Beach noted the lowest incidence of copulation among the Keraki, who generaly have (had) sexual intercourse only once a week. The Lesu do a little better with once or twice a week. Two or three times a week is thought to be typical among the Chiricahua and the Trukese. More active still, the Hopi Indians were reckoned to copulate three or four times a week; and "although the Crow

Indians think it weakening to have intercourse every night, they find it difficult to do so less frequently." Among the Siriono, coitus usually occurs about once a day. The Aranda of Australia were said to have sexual intercourse as much as five times nightly, sleeping between each sex act. And the Ifugao of the Philippines were reckoned to admire men who had intercourse several times in a single night. The African Thonga male may copulate with three or four of his wives in a single night, as already noted; and Chagga males have surprising virility. I have come across no records among whites to equal the Chagga accomplishments.

Most frequent ejaculation on one occasion

The majority of men manage one ejaculation when called upon. Some – mostly the younger ones – manage a second within a short space of time. A fewer number manage a third or a fourth. In a tiny minority of cases a man may achieve an even greater number of orgasms and accompanying ejaculations. The highest number of ejaculations I have seen reliably reported (Kinsey) is the 6 to 8 accomplished by a 39-year-old Negro male on a single occasion. This hardly compares with the high numbers achieved for *orgasmic* frequency, but it should always be remembered that orgasm can occur without the discharge of seminal fluid.

Farthest projected ejaculation

This, we may assume, is yet another one for a future Sex Olympics. Considering the amount of masturbation that goes on there must be considerable volume of semen discharged in the absence of a convenient vaginal receptacle. The distances the seminal fluid achieves before being arrested in flight must surely vary. I have seen very little documentation on this. Van de Velde notes that the "rhythmic spasms of ejaculation fling forth the semen from the external orifice with an impetus which may be perceived if the emission takes place *in vacuo.*" He adds, with the air of the true scientist, that the "seminal stream usually covers a distance of from 15 to 20 cm., but has been known to exceed 1 m.".

Tom Johnston

Oldest productive man
In the average human ejaculate there are several hundred million live and mobile sperm. The older a man gets the fewer sperm he manages to manufacture. By the age of eighty or ninety most men are infertile, though they often have enjoyable sex-lives. In a few relatively isolated communities old men appear to sire offspring with great success, a facility that appears to be associated with great longevity – as, for instance, in Georgia in the USSR and in the valley of Vilcabamba in Ecuador. I have yet to see studies of fertility in old men in these communities. The oldest man I have seen quoted as still producing live sperm is mentioned by Havelock Ellis – "the sperm-secreting function has no necessary final term and may be continued to advanced old age, even in one reported case to the age of 103." See "Physiology of Sex" by H. Ellis.

Maximum production capacity in males
Writers are notoriously vague about the number of human sperm produced. It doesn't matter too much – when you are dealing in hundreds of millions of the little fellows the odd few million are not all that important. One writer suggests that the number of human sperm can vary from zero to 700 million or more per millilitre. The zero bit needn't surprise us: after all we know that some men are sterile. The upper extreme, however, is quite remarkable. Considering the complexity of a single sperm the capabilities of the testes in generating such intricate machines by the hundreds of million are little short of miraculous.

Most copious human ejaculation
Penis size has always worried human males more than ejaculate volume – though if more men read pornography they may enlarge their ambitions. Van de Velde suggests in "Ideal Marriage" that human semen, in one ejaculation, can be as much as 10 ml. Though G. I. M. Swyer sets his sights higher – "volumes up to 15 ml. have been recorded". Walter (again of "My Secret Life") mentions a harlot who "knew a man who spent a dessert-spoonful". It's not an area that men have tended to boast about, though in certain forms of literature a copious discharge is a definite point in the hero's favour. In pornography there is frequently talk of veritable "lakes of sperm," a state of affairs that is not all that likely to arouse ordinary folk to efforts of emulation.

Most common type of impotence
There is dispute as to whether premature ejaculation should be counted an instance of impotence. It is evidently a sign of male inadequacy and is commoner than, say, erectile impotence. Kinsey however refused to recognize premature ejaculation as a problem for the male, though it evidently caused distress to a woman. Kinsey noted, in justification, that many mammals ejaculate very rapidly. Some sexologists have retorted that premature ejaculation is definitely a problem for the man. Thus Brecher remarks that "It seems to me very clear that on this point Kinsey was quite wrong. The later Masters-Johnson studies of premature ejaculation reveal in precisely what respects he was wrong."

41

"Impotence" first used

The word is derived from the Latin impotentia (lit: lack of power). In 1420 the word was used in a poem "De regimine Principum" by Thomas Hoccleve (c. 1370-1454) to mean "want of strength" or "helplessness", "Hir impotence, Strecchith naght so fer as his influence". In another poem, "La male regle", of the same period, the word is used in the sense of "want of physical power or feebleness": "As I said, reeve on impotence that likely am to serve yit or eeue". But the use of the word to mean loss of sexual power first occurred in 1655 in Church History of Britain by Thomas Fuller (1608-61): "Whilest Papists crie up this, his incredible Incontinency: others uneasily unwonder the same by imputing it partly to Impotence afflicted, by an infirmitie."

First clinical description of impotence

The first clinical definition appears in Copland's "Dictionary of Practical Medicine" in editions between 1833 and 1858. Later Strauss (1950) defines it as "the inability to perform the sexual act". Ernest Jones (1918) declares it is "the complete or incomplete inability satisfactorily to carry out heterosexual coitus per vaginam. Satisfactorily means adequate erection, time and control of ejaculation."

Most coital positions in sex manual

Most sex manuals, past and present, do not enumerate more than forty or fifty coital positions – and much depends upon semantics. Here again there are few ground rules. If, for example, you shift a leg a couple of inches does it count as a new position? In one nineteenth-century work a sexologist, D. K. Forberg, claimed that there were no less than ninety positions for sexual intercourse. This has been claimed as one of the highest estimates ever made. As a note to "The Perfumed Garden" Walter remarks that Forberg restricts himself to the positions assumed in ancient Greece and Rome. Presumably if only slight variations in position qualified as a different kind we could think of literally hundreds of coital possibilities.

Most coital positions in Chinese sex manual

In a famous Chinese sex manual, the "Art of the Bedchamber", a Taoist named Tung Hsuan Tzu developed the theories and instructions left behind by earlier sex instructors – such as Lady Purity, Lady Mystery, the Yellow Emperor and Peng Tsu. He begins his work – "Of all human behaviour, intercourse is most sublime ..." He discusses thirty positions for sexual intercourse – based on the nine methods

of Lady Mystery, though with more variety. The coital positions carry pleasant titles, such as The Cuddling Chat, The Passionate Narration, The Fish Exposes Its Gills, The Unicorn Shows Its Horn. The Silkworms Entwine, The Dragon Swings, etc. In addition to the named positions, he also discusses a further twenty-eight positions, making a grand total of fifty-eight coital possibilities.

Least number of coital positions in sex manual

In his best-selling book "Ideal Marriage" Van de Gelde lists only ten "possible" positions. These range from the normal or habitual posture with the woman supine to the "equitation" method of Martial where the woman sits astride the man and faces him. Each position is described in detail with attention given to the stimulation afforded in each case.

Most popular coital positions in marriage

In the Kinsey surveys it was shown, hardly surprisingly, that the commonest position for marital coitus was with the male above. All the females questioned gave this as the usual position.

Least popular coital positions in marriage

Only four per cent of women surveyed by Kinsey employed a standing position for marital coitus; and only about one in ten tried sexual intercourse in a sitting position – about the same percentage that *only* had intercourse with the man above.

Most popular pre-marital coital positions

As we may expect, pre-marital coitus usually happened with the man above the woman and the woman on her back. Marriage did not affect this situation in people surveyed by Kinsey. It did, however, affect the willingness to experiment. The man above/woman below was the *only* position for 21 per cent of unmarrieds but only nine per cent of marrieds.

Least popular pre-marital coital positions

As with married couples, standing among pre-marrieds was the least likely position for sexual intercourse (four per cent). Rear entry coitus was only slightly more likely (six per cent) among pre-married couples, though marrieds rated fifteen per cent. Marriage does not, apparently, affect the eagerness with which sitting coitus is embarked upon (eight per cent pre-marrieds, nine per cent marrieds). The figures, inevitably, can be interpreted in many ways. Do married couples enjoy sex more and so learn to give their coitus a wide-ranging richness? Or do they simply experiment to hold off marital boredom as long as possible? Possibly any generalization is unwise.

Sexiest weddings

The wedding ritual has been accompanied, from one society to another, by a wide range of coital activities. In various countries feudal lords were apparently entitled to deflower the young bride before releasing her to her husband. This "right of the first night" (*jus primae noctis*), known also in France as *jus cunni* and in England as *marchette,* appears to have been established on the historical evidence. Monks sometimes held the right: thus the monks of St. Thiodard enjoyed this right over the inhabitants of Mount Auriol. More extraordinarily, in some tradition, e.g. the Nasamonian custom, all the wedding guests are expected to copulate with the bride. The kiss given the bride by men present at an English wedding is a poor relation of this old custom.

Highest sexual expenses incurred

Louis XV of France, a man of prodigious sexual appetite, established a royal harem in the Parc aux Cerfs; the house was situated in the grounds of Versailles. The local garrison was charged with the task of preventing local young men penetrating the secrets of the harem. And a certain Mère Bompart served the king as procuress. The cost of maintaining this institution was high. Some of the major items – apart from board and lodging on a luxurious scale – were indemnities paid to families, dowries for those who were married off, the maintenance of illegitimate children, presents to the élèves, and the particular expense of Mère Bompart. It has been estimated that in the thirty-four years of its existence the Parc aux Cerfs cost nearly 20 million dollars, or around $600,000 a year – a lot to pay for the sexual pleasures of one man.

Most extreme male promiscuity

In a field where lovers incline to boast it is always difficult to ascertain the truth. Kinsey found very few men or women who had had more than one hundred sexual partners. Historically, however, a number of performers have notched up a much higher figure than this. Some tales are perhaps too legendary to believe. For example, Conchobar, the King of Ulster in the twelfth century, was said (in the ancient "Book of Leinster") to have slept with all the marriagable girls in the kingdom. Perhaps more reliably, the nineteenth-century Walter is said to have slept with a thousand or two women: the Kronhausens in "Walter the English Casanova" remark that he admitted making love "to at least one thousand two hundred women;" and Brecher in "An Analysis of Human Sexual Response", talks of Walter having an "estimated two thousand women." Perhaps Don Juan – with "his personal tally of 2,065 conquests" – is the record holder. (See J. Atkins' "Sex in Literature")

Most extreme female promiscuity

In the Kinsey survey only 1 per cent of women had, for example, pre-marital coitus with as many as twenty-odd different partners. Yet the same percentage of men had pre-marital coitus with more than a hundred different partners. Kinsey accepts "the male's greater inclination to be promiscuous" yet this belief is going beyond the data. Perhaps, for instance, women desire wide sexual relationships as much as men but are more inhibited or lack the opportunities, a consequence of male-orientated society. Anyway a number of historical performers – Cleopatra, Messalina, etc. – are quite as impressive as the men. The record is surely held by Madame de Saint-Ange, who argued that a woman can be ruined by lovers but that mere acts of libertinism are quickly forgotten – "That is the conduct I would always prescribe to all women who would follow in my steps. In the twelve years I have been married I have been had by perhaps ten or twelve thousand individuals." (Quoted in J. Atkins' "Sex in Literature".)

Most sexually athletic Arab

There is a view of lore that it is based on fact. Be that as it may, it is certainly true that the Arabs traditionally admired great sexual prowess, esteeming highly the most prodigious performers. In "The Fabulous Feats of the Futtering Freebooters" the value of hemp is celebrated as causing the jade-stick to "become as hard as iron and hot as fire, fit for intercourse with a hundred girls." The penis of Abu'l-Haylukh remained in erection for thirty days; Abu'l-Hayjeh deflowered eighty virgins in one night; Felah the Negro "did jerk off his yard for all of a week;" the Negro Maymun made "sixty days of coition his score. . . ." etc., etc., (quoted in A. Edwardes & R. E. L. Masters, "The Cradle of Erotica").

Most sexually athletic in the West

We have already mentioned some prodigious Western performers. To their names may be added Casanova ("Memoires") and Frank Harris ("My Life and Loves"). Guy de Maupassant was said to suffer from satyriasis or chronic hyperexcitability of the penis – sometimes taken as the male equivalent of nymphomania. Maupassant told Frank Harris that he could make love half a dozen times in a single hour; later he made the same boast to Flaubert and, to prove his point, went to

a brothel with a witness and accomplished the trick. Maupassant claimed to be no more tired after making love twenty times than after two!

Most sexually athletic in China

The Emperor Yang Ti of the Sui Dynasty (A.D. 581-617) was foremost in inventing and indulging sexual pleasures. After various military adventures he settled down to pursue amorous intrigue. He enjoyed one queen, two deputy queens, six royal consorts and seventy-two royal madames. There were also 3,000 palace maidens, hand-picked by special envoys throughout the land; and he included two of his late father's concubines in his harem. In particular he attached importance to novel ways of making love. When he travelled, he took with him a caravan of ten special chariots: in each a naked beauty lay on heavily padded red satin, awaiting his favour.

Guy de Maupassant, above, made love to half a dozen ladies in the space of one hour. Below, the Italian adventurer, Casanova, lives up to his prodigious reputation.

Most famous male celibate

It has been said of a number of famous people that they never experienced sexual intercourse. It is hard to establish such claims as the truth. It was said that Im-

Immanuel Kant, a virgin at 80

Catherine the Great, "of questionable morals"

Empress's English physician, Mr. Rogerson, and by Miss Protas, the royal *éprouveuse*. The function of the latter was to test out the sexual abilities of potential favourites. All, apparently, was successful and Zubof was duly installed.

manual Kant, the German philosopher, died a virgin at the age of eighty. And the allegation was made that Sir Isaac Newton never experienced sexual intercourse. "Although mathematical genius can hardly be attributed to this singular neglect on Sir Isaac's part, it might certainly explain why he suffered so severely from insomnia." (B. J. Hurwood, "The Golden Age of Erotica.")

Most sexually vigorous Czarina

This, we all know, was Catherine of Russia, a woman of inexhaustible sexual appetite. Foot-tickling and bottom-slapping gave her particular sexual delight, and people were employed for these purposes. Even late in life this doughty Czarina was persistently seeking out new thrills. When she was sixty she fancied a young lieutenant in the horseguards, named Plato Zubof aged twenty-five. He was duly inspected by the

Earliest "Playboy King" in China

King Chou-hsin of the Shang dynasty (1558-1302 B.C.) has been represented as the first "playboy king" in Chinese history. He was said to be more than eight feet in height, the tallest man in his kingdom; he was described by one historian as a man "with a back as strong as that of a tiger and a waist comparable to that of a bear." He was said to kill tigers and leopards with his bare hands. Night after night, so it is said, he would cope with "ten healthy and strong women in a row" without any sign of contentment. One trick was to order a naked woman to entwine her legs round his waist: virtually supporting her on his erect member he would then walk round the room.

Most sexually active Caesar

Various Roman Caesars indulged themselves in a wide range of sexual pursuits. Nero and Caligula, for instance, were known for their orgies, sexual appetites, and "perverted" pleasures. Tiberius, perhaps, has the edge over them all. Throughout his life he indulged in all manner of sexual behaviour; and even in old age he contrived a private sporting-house in which all forms of sexual behaviour would be performed in front of him. Young boys, whom he called his "minnows", would move between his legs while he was swimming, to lick and tease his penis. Sometimes he even used unweaned babies to suck him – "such a filthy old man he had become!" ("The Twelve Caesars", Suetonius). He also collected erotica – pictures, sculpture, and erotic manuals from Elephantis in Egypt. One story is that when an acolyte and his brother, the sacred trumpeter, would not submit to his pleasure he assaulted them and then had their legs broken.

Most sexually active Popes

The Papacy has a startling sexual history. Pope Sergius III arranged, with the help of his mother, that his bastard should become Pope after him. John XII, deposed in A.D. 963, turned St. John Lateran into a brothel: he was accused of adultery and incest. Leo VIII, who replaced him, died stricken in paralysis in the act of adultery. Benedict IX, elected Pope at the age of ten, grew up "in unrestrained license, and shocked the sensibilities even of a dull and barbarous age." Balthasar Cossa, elected Pope to end the Great Schism, later admitted to incest, adultery, and other crimes ("two hundred maids, matrons and widows, including a few nuns, fell victims to his brutal lust"). In one famous occurrence at the court of Pope Alexander VI, prostitutes were called to dance naked before the assembly, after which prizes were offered to those men who, in the opinion of the spectators, managed to copulate with the most number of prostitutes.

Most virgins deflowered in a year

We recorded Abu'l Hayjeh who deflowered eighty virgins in a single night, but we may suspect that real possibilities lie elsewhere. The upper classes in eighteenth-century England developed a veritable obsession for deflowering virgins, and men boasted of their virility by claiming many conquests of this sort. One

man claimed to have debauched no less than seventy girls in a single year (See B. Walker, "Sex and the Supernatural"). One purpose of the notorious Hellfire Clubs – devoted to drunkenness, wenching, group sex, etc. – was to provide a ready supply of virgin girls.

Most famous dilatory Royal husband

Louis XIII of France married Anne of Austria when both were only fourteen years old. On their wedding night they spent two hours together with nurses in attendance. Louis apparently *pretended* to satisfaction, saying that he had consummated twice. Then – despite the urgings of the entourage, the confessor and the cardinal – he refused to attempt the sex act again until three years later. After a further three years the Queen miscarried. Some time later Louis XIV was born.

Most famous use of a biblical virgin

The most celebrated use of a biblical virgin was the effort to rejuvenate the senile King David (1 Kings 1, 1–4). David was "old and stricken in years," and so his servants thought that a virgin might help – "let her cherish him, and let her lie in thy bosom, that my Lord the king may get heat." They sought for "a fair damsel throughout all the coasts of Israel ... the damsel was very fair, and cherished the king, and ministered to him: but the king knew her not." Adonijah, the son of Haggith, was not sorry: he declared "I will be king." 47

Happiest sex-role reversal communities

The Arapesh and Mundugumor tribes, described by Margaret Mead, agree in making little differentiation on a sex role basis. Differences that occur between individuals are not "sex-linked." A third tribe studied by Mead offers an example of a clear case of sex role reversal between men and women. This occurred among the Tchambuli partly as a result of the imposition of the "Pax Britannica", which outlawed tribal wars. The warriors lost their traditional role and became largely decorative in society. The economic support of the society still depended upon the women and their status, in consequence, improved. In the words of one commentator – ". . . the woman emerges as the dominant, impersonal managing partner, secure and cooperative, while the man develops into a less responsible and emotionally dependant person, prone to petty bickering and misunderstandings." Sex role reversal, insofar as it affects parental function, has also been noted among the Manus.

Most streakers at one time

The University of Maryland claimed to have mustered no less than 553 naked students to streak three miles one evening in March 1974. This beats the record claimed by the University of South Carolina of 508 a few nights earlier. These efforts, however, are paltry compared with the 1,000 claimed by the students at Athens, Georgia, or the 1,200 claimed in Boulder, Colorado ("Economist", March 16, 1974). (Perhaps most remarkable about the streaking fashion is the hysteria with which it has been greeted in some judicial and press circles. Yet again we are led to believe that the human body is inherently obscene, a judgment that is reflected in some of the penalties on offending streakers. In one instance in Britain a streaker, harmless enough, was fined £100; in another instance, in Belfast, a streaker was sent to jail for three months!)

SEX AIDS

Oldest sex aid

When we survey all the sex aid paraphernalia in the modern magazines we may be forgiven for thinking that such things are a product of modern "permissiveness." Clearly the ancient Romans did not have the opportunity to play around with electronic vibrators – but they had a variety of gadgets that have hardly been surpassed today. And even older peoples have used sex aid devices, e.g. dildoes. In sculptures from ancient Babylon a dildo (artificial penis) is clearly shown, and such implements were equally common in Ancient Indian China, and elsewhere (I. Block, "Sexual Life in England"). And the elaborate dildoes mentioned in Ezekiel XVI, 17 ("Thou hast also taken thy fair jewels of my gold and of my silver, which I had given thee, and madest to thyself images of men, and didst commit whoredom with them") may surprise a few people acquainted only with Sunday School scripture.

Earliest account of the origin of the dildo

Several accounts of the origin of the dildo have been published in Britain and elsewhere. The earliest thorough-going attempt is taken by one writer to be the "Wonderful and Edifying History of the Origin of the Godemiché or Dildo" printed at the end of an erotic work The Schoolfellows; or Young Ladies Guide to Love (London, 1830). The account is a translation from L'Histoire merveilleuse et édifiante du Godemiché in the second part of "L'Aretin ou la Débauche de l'Esprit of Abbé Dulaurens" (Rome, 1763 and 1768).

First English account of the dildo in action

According to one authority the earliest account of a dildo in action in the English language is to be found in "The Choise of Valentines or the Merie Ballad of Nash his Dildo". Nashe lived from 1567-1601: a detailed account, from this period, of a "deviate" sexual act is very rare.

First sex aid recommended in China

The first explicit recommendation of sex aids – as opposed to their age-old use – in China was made by Buddhist monks who urged the use of sex instruments during the reign of Empress Wu Tse-T'ien (A.D. 1685-1704). Historical records show that the imperial physician, Ming Ch'ung-yen presented the Empress with a sex aid

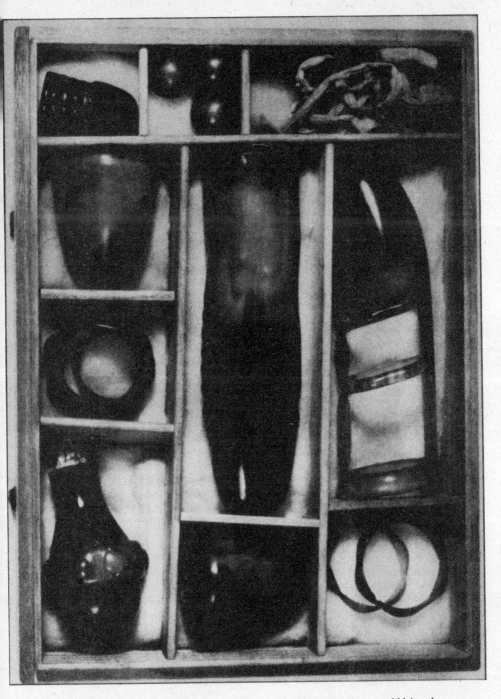

A Japanese "Happy Box". Note the tortoiseshell condom (used also as a dildo) and those little brass balls with bells inside which women would wear inside their vaginas to orchestrate the sexual act.

called a "live limb" for her amusement in the royal bedchamber. The device, made of rubber, was brought to the imperial capital by a Buddhist monk from India via Tibet. A full description is found in a Chinese version of one of the Buddhist classics (E. Chou, "The Dragon and the Phoenix") – a nun, having "the need," has a "live limb" manufactured for her use – "When it was ready, the nun took it with her into the inner room. She tied the rubber live limb to her ankle and pushed it inside her by bending her knee and moving her foot so that her carnal desire was satisfied."

The happy ring first introduced
The "happy ring," also known as the "goat's eyelid," was first introduced to the Mongol Emperors by Tibetan lamas in the thirteenth century. After a goat was killed its eyelids were removed together with the eyelashes. First they were put in quick-lime to dry; then they were steamed in a bamboo basket for not less than twelve hours — this procedure was repeated several times. Once completed the process yielded a sex aid that could be tied round the penis (jade-stem) prior to coitus. The goat's eyelashes were supposed to give the woman a pleasant tickling sensation. Modern versions of the "goat's eyelid" – usually made of plastic – can be found in sex aid shops in this country and elsewhere.

Most celebrated Chinese sex aid
The Orient was prolific in its sex aids. Perhaps the most famous of the Chinese love instruments was the silver clasp. Clamped about the base of the penis, its purpose was to prolong erection by preventing the blood from leaving the engorged organ. The Japanese "pleasure ring" has a similar purpose. Elastic bands can accomplish the same purpose.

Most popular type of dildo
Throughout history the most popular dildos have always been those that occurred in nature, i.e. fruit and veg. Carrots, bananas etc. have always been employed by frustrated – and not so frustrated – women as substitute penises.

Of artificial devices the candle is perhaps the most widely used. John Atkins quotes "execrable verse" by Suckling –

There is a thing which in the light
Is seldom us'd; but in the night
It serves the female maiden crew,
The ladies and the good-wives too:
They use to take in their hand,
And then it will uprightly stand;
And to a hole they it apply,
Where by its goodwill it would die;
It spends, goes out, and still within
It leaves its moisture thick and thin.

There are candle episodes in various fictional works, e.g. in Apollinaire's "Memories of a Young Rakehell", Miller's "Sexus", etc.

Most drastic sex aid
Dissatisfaction with the penis as a sexual tool has led men to a variety of measures for its improvement. Some of these would seem to be rather hazardous. The Malays of Borneo, for instance, are reported in F. Henriques' "Love in Action" as perforating the penis with brass wire spread out at the ends – soley to aid titillation of the vagina. Sometimes bamboo, ivory, or silver rods, with metal balls at the ends, can be used in the same way (Norman Haire, "The Encyclopaedia of Sex Practice"). Among the Malays the device is known as ampallang, palang, untang, campion. The Bataks of Sumatra actually insert lumps of stone into wounds made in the penis. When the wounds heal, the penis is lumpy, thus supposedly giving more pleasure to the woman in coitus.

Vibrators – least expected consequences
Plastic vibrators, generally used by women as a dildo device, can also be employed by men, e.g. by homosexuals – sometimes with strange results. In a letter to the "British Medical Journal," June 30, 1974, two writers from London's St. Bartholomew's Hospital bring to the attention of readers "a new physical sign". Within the space of a fortnight two patients were admitted through the accident and emergency department "with a painful vibrating umbilicus". Both the patients were young homosexuals, aged 19 and 25 years, who were accustomed to using battery-

This advertisement is to inform our customers and others, that the woman who pretended the name of Philips, in Orange-court, is now dead, and that the business is carried on at

Mrs. PHILIPS's WAREHOUSE,

That has been for forty years, at the Green Canister, in Bedford (late Half-Moon) Street, seven doors from the Strand, on the left hand side,

STILL continues in its original state of reputation; where all gentlemen of intrigue may be supplied with those Bladder Policies, or implements of safety, which infallibly secure the health of our customers, superior in quality as has been demonstrated in comparing samples of others that pretend the name of *Philips*; we defy any one to equal our goods in England, and have lately had several large orders from France, Spain, Portugal, Italy, and other foreign places.

N. B. Ambassadors, foreigners, gentlemen and captains of ships, &c. going abroad, may be supplied with any quantity of the best goods in England, on the shortest notice and lowest price. A most infamous and obscene hand-bill, or advertisement, in the name of *Philips* is false: the public are hereby assured that their name is not *Philips*, but this is her shop, and the same person is behind the counter as has been for many years.——The following lines are very applicable to our goods :

To gard yourself from shame or fear,
Votaries to Venus, hasten here;
None in our wares e'er found a flaw,
Self-preservation's nature's law.
Letters (post paid) duly answered.

There were actually two Mrs. Phillipses in London, both claiming to be unique sex aid retailers. Here is an advertisement for one of them.

operated stimulators or vibrators. What had happened was that the vibrators had been lost into the rectum through the anus, apparently at the moment of orgasm. Apart from the vibrating umbilicus, a cylindrical mass could be felt arising from the pelvis and a gentle hum could be heard. The vibrator was removed from one patient easily enough but the other required a general anaesthetic.

Most famous 18th-century sex-aid retailer
A certain Mrs. Phillips, in eighteenth century London, operated a sex aid shop "unique in the world". – "It consists of wares which are never sold publicly, which indeed can hardly be found at all in ordinary towns, and are only made and used in London and Paris. In Paris they are sold secretly in fancy shops; in London this woman has a shop near Leicester Square with them as her only wares."

51

Part III

The Arts

BOOKS
Oldest sex manual
The oldest sex manuals in the world can be traced to China, more than two and a half thousand years before the birth of Christ. Huang-Ti (2697-2598 B.C.), the legendary Yellow Emperor, has been regarded as the originator of the traditional sex practices and beliefs. The ancient "Handbooks of Sex," composed nearly five thousand years ago, anticipate anything produced in the West by well over two thousand years.

Most famous sex manual in Rome
Ovid wrote his "Ars Amatoria" (The Art of Love) about the time of Christ. One writer (H. Montgomery Hyde in "A History of Pornography") has characterized the book as an "immoral book" representing the art of love as "the adulterer's art rather than the husband's art." Renaissance humanists praised the book. It begins with the words – "If anyone among this people know not the art of loving let him read my poem, and having read be skilled in love. By skill swift ships are sailed and rowed, by skill nimble chariots are driven: by skill must love be guided."

Most prolific Chinese writers
In the Eastern Han Dynasty (A.D. 25-220), a group of Taoist philosophers created Yin Taoism, firmly rooted in the importance of human sexual expression. This school of Taoists wrote volume after volume of sex manuals including "Su Nu Ching" (Manual of Lady Purity), "Yu Fang Mi Chueh" (Secret Codes of the Jade Room), the "Art of the Bedchamber" and "Yu Fang Chih Yao" (Important Guidelines of the Jade Room). To give their works authority and to exert influence on the emperors the Yin Taoists attributed the key points in their manuals to Huang Ti (the Yellow Emperor) and the ancient authority Peng Tsu who was said to have lived to 800 years of age.

Oldest Indian sex manual
The oldest and best known Indian sex manual is the "Kama Sutra of Vatsyayana", written about 1500 years ago. It has been pointed out that this comprehensive volume summarized many earlier writings on sexual topics dating back as much as three thousand years. The first English edition of the "Kama Sutra" was privately printed in 1883; the Indian "Ananga-Ranga" (or "The Stage of Love", also known as "Kamaled-hiplava" or "A Boat in the Ocean of Love") was translated into English ten years before the "Kama Sutra". This latter, more important work, is the first full manual from India devoted exclusively to the subject of human sexuality and in particular to the relationships between the sexes.

First Indian sex manual translated into English
The "Ananga-Ranga", published three-quarters of the way through the nineteenth century, was to have appeared as "The Kama Sutra", or "The Hindoo Art of Love". Alas, the printer, after reading the galleys, lost his nerve and refused to go on with the job. A consequence is that the proof copies in existence are extremely rare. Arbuthnot and Richard Burton translated the "Ananga-Ranga" – which was not written by a holy man (as was the 'Kama Sutra") but by a poet named Kalyana Mall. It has been published into many languages under a variety of titles – "The Pleasures of Women", "The Form of the Bodiless One", "The Writ of Desire" etc

Most important sex manual in medieval India
In the words of one jacket blurb: the "Koka Shastra" (Trans. A. Comfort, Allen & Unwin, 1964) and its associated texts are to medieval literature what the "Kama Sutra' was to ancient. When Kokkoka turned in the twelfth century to the themes of love and sex the move was audacious: for a thousand years the "Kama Sutra" representing the summed wisdom of earlier times, had been supreme. What more was there to say? Medieval India was different to the India of Vatsyayana. "A new approach was needed yet the early pages suggest that we are reading a new abridgement of the classic work, a sibling rather than a sequel." And Kokkoka frequently expresses his debt to the earlier

Right: "Bull Among Cows" from the Kama Sutra

master. The abiding value of the Sanskrit texts, as of many other ancient works, is the positive attitude to human sexuality.

First manual to deduce sexual attributes from a woman's face

According to "Yu Fang Mi Chueh" ("Secret Codes of the Jade Room"), a Taoist sex manual written not long after the birth of Christ, it is possible to judge a woman's sexual features by scrutinising her face – "A woman with a small mouth and short fingers has a shallow porte feminine and she is easy to please. You can be sure that a woman must have big and thick labia if she has a big mouth and thick lips. If she has deep-set eyes, her porte feminine is bound to be deep too . . . if a woman has a pair of big, sparkling eyes, her porte feminine is narrow at its entrance, and yet roomy in the inner part . . . A woman with two dimples is tight and narrow down below . . ." etc., etc. It is interesting to note that some of the superstitions of ancient Chinese are current in modern Western society.

Highest circulation sex manual

In this permissive age it may come as a surprise to many that perhaps the best selling sex technique book of them all was first published in 1926. Written simultaneously in Dutch and German, and quickly translated into many languages, "Ideal Marriage" by Theodoor Hendrik van de Velde (1873-1937) went through forty-two printings in Germany alone between 1926 and 1932: it was suppressed in 1933 when Hitler came to power. By the 1970s the English translation, published by William Heinemann in 1930, had gone through forty-three printings totalling an estimated 700,000 copies. In America more than half-a-million hardcover copies had been sold between 1945 and 1970; a revised edition was published in 1965.

Most comprehensive modern manual

The most comprehensive of modern sex manuals is "The Joy of Sex" by Alex Comfort. A subtitle on the book is "A Gourmet Guide to Love Making." Thirty-two colour prints are included and more

han a hundred black and white illustrations. In *The Washington Post* Anthony Storr rather pompously remarked that "... the illustrations, of which there are many, are frankly beautiful and entirely lack that kind of surreptitious, suggestive titillation that characterizes pornography."

First exposé of sex in the confessional

The Roman Catholic confessional has often intrigued those who have little or no experience of it and some of those who have an intimate acquaintance with the device. From time to time exposés have appeared of what actually takes place in the confessional; after all, in more dis-

Above: Alex Comfort, author of "The Joy of Sex"

"The Monk and the Dairy Maid" 19th c. bronze

solute times the confessional was used by randy priests as a means of recruiting likely women. In the nineteenth century a number of publications, mostly of poor quality, appeared claiming to reveal what went on in nunneries, monasteries and the confessional. One such was the "Awful Disclosures of Maria Monk": the author claimed to have been a nun in the *Hotel Dieu* in Montreal. Her disclosures, first printed in New York in 1836, were reprinted again and again in the U.S. and Europe, and by 1851 more than a quarter of a million copies of the book were in circulation. A leading Catholic called the book "blasphemous fiction" and it was mentioned during debates in Parliament. In 1874 a certain Father Chiniquy published a book called "The Priest, The Woman, and the Confessional:" harrowing accounts were given of sex in the confessional. A more sensational book had appeared in London ten years earlier – "The Confessional Unmasked: showing the Depravity of the Romish Priesthood, the iniquity of the Confessional and the Questions Put to Females in Confession."

Largest sex book collections
There are sex books and sex books! There is all the difference betwen a piece of cheap nineteenth-century pornography and a detailed research publication in sexology. Prudes have often failed to make a distinction, and when a distinction has been attempted it has often been bogus. The biggest sex book collections in the world contain *all* types of sexual literature – from the simply titillating to the driest scholarly tome. The leading sex institutes – associated with the names of Bloch, Hirschfeld, etc. – all had associated libraries. The Kinsey Institute (more properly The Institute for Sex Research) has around 20,000 books of all sorts as does the British Museum. According to H. Montgomery Hyde, the Vatican Library tops them all with something like 25,000 volumes.

Longest title
We have already met a number of book titles that seem needlessly lengthy. The longest I have come across is the one by Schurig (it is apparently typical of his book titles in general) –

"*MULIEBRIA Historico-Medica, hoc est Partium Genitalium Muliebrium Consideratio Physico-Medico-Forensis, qua Pudendi Muliebris Partes tam externae, quam internae, scilicet Uterus cum Ipsi Annexis Ovariis et Tubis Fallopianis, nec non Varia de Clitoride et Tribadismo de Hymen et Nymphotomania seu Feminarum Circumsisione et Castratione selectis et curiosis observationibus traduntur.*" A. D. Martino Schurigio, Physico Dresdensi . . . MDCCXXIX.

After which you may feel there is little point in reading the book!

Largest human penis in fiction
In fiction and legend the human penis can be any size. Malinowski wrote of the Legend of Inuvayla'u, who was the head of his clan and possessed of a remarkably long organ. When the women of the tribe were cleaning the ground or weeding he would stand behind a fence and push his penis through a convenient aperture. It would wriggle along the ground like a snake, and when the women went bathing the penis would chase them through the water like an eel. Eventually he left the village, before he went cutting off his penis and testicles: they turned to stone as they fell. The testicles can still be seen, as large round boulders; and the glans penis is a pointed helmet-shaped piece of coral. In the "Arabian Nights" many vast organs are paraded. In one of the stories there is a description of a *zabb*, "as great as an ass's or an elephant's, a powerful sight to see." In another of the stories a man is able to wish for a large penis, whereupon the zabb grew enormously until it resembled a calabash lying between two pumpkins. The weight was so great that the poor fellow could no longer stand. And at a more mundane level we have the straightforward exaggerations common in pornographic fiction of all ages. In de Sade's "The 120 Days of Sodom" Hercule boasts a 13 in. long penis. In Chinese fiction there are similarly impressive items of equipment, with organs invariably described as of "incredible length," "bigger than a sea cucumber" or "too thick to be encircled by a lady's fingers." The hardness of such monsters was comparable to that of an iron post, and such

organs could support, when erect, a bushel of wheat hung from the end!

Earliest penis transplant in fiction

In a seventeenth-century Chinese tale, *Jou-pu-t'uan*, there is an account of a penis transplant, or, perhaps more accurately, a penis graft. A Scholar inquires of the Master of Medicine how a gigantic organ can be acquired. One technique, as carefully explained, is to make use of the erect organ of a dog. It is arranged for the dog and bitch to copulate; in the midst of the act the Master of Medicine cuts off the penis of the dog and, slicing it up, inserts the parts into the incised organ of the man requiring a larger member – "With luck, there will be a perfect grafting of man and dog."

Most frequent male orgasm in fiction

Some literary accounts of sexual experience may or may not be true. It is not a field where men are apt to be modest. Boswell gives us a nice account in his "London Journal". In one encounter, which took place with Louisa on 12 January 1763, he was "fairly lost in supreme rapture" no less than five times, and the worthy Louisa declared him a prodigy. Atkins suggests that "Boswell was probably truthful."

Debate about frequency of orgasm often centres on six or seven times as remarkable. In literature there are many examples around such figures – in *Teleny*, "As true votaries of the Grecian god, we poured out seven copious libations to Priapus." In *Catullus*, a bigger figure is mentioned –

> . . . and bid some servant bar the door;
> and don't rush out to call or shop,
> but nicely wait for what I'll bring,
> and then – nine hugs without a stop!

And Ovid, though growing old, managed it nine times with Corinna – but he is not at

all satisfied. In de Sade's *Juliette*, Minsky never goes to bed without first discharging ten times ("It is a fact that the inordinate amount of human flesh I eat contributes greatly to the augmentation and thickening of my seminal fluid"). Such men are weaklings compared with the performers of Arab and Japanese legend. In the "Arabian Nights" one man manages to make love forty times in one night; Japanese sexual athletes are similarly insatiable. And there is a pleasant little joke I cannot resist including – An English sailor got into an argument with a Chinese sailor in Shanghai, each boasting how many times he could do it. They decided to put the matter to the test. Each took a girl to bed. The Englishman performed once, then again, and finally – with difficulty for he had drunk too much – a third time. He marked each one on the wall with an upright stroke. In the morning the exhausted Chinese crawled into his room. He looked at the Englishman's tally and exclaimed – "One hundred and eleven! Beaten by one, by God!"

60

Richard Burton holds the record as the most prolific sex translator.

Most prolific sex translator
Sir Richard Francis Burton (1821–87) was one of the most accomplished and many-sided men of the nineteenth century. As well as being a man of action (explorer, swordsman, etc.) he possessed immense intellectual ability – as ethnologist, linguist, poet, amateur botanist, zoologist, and geologist. He published forty-three volumes describing his travels, two volumes of poetry, and more than one hundred articles. In particular he translated sixteen volumes of the "Arabian Nights", six volumes of Portugese literature, two volumes of Latin poetry, four volumes of folklore (Neapolitan, African and Hindu), etc. In the words of his (perhaps) most skilful biographer (F. M Brodie, "The Devil Drives") "...Burton was no ordinary translator; the inflexible integrity, brilliance, and vigour of his translations are an index to the man himself. One stands in awe of the ease

"Have you any pornography suitable for an elderly maiden aunt?"

with which he moved from Hindustani for his "Pilpay's Fables" and "Vikram and Vampire" – to Portuguese for his "Camoens" and "Lacerda" – to Arabic for the "Arabian Nights" and the "Perfumed Garden" – to Neapolitan Italian for his "Il Pentamerone" – to Sanscrit for his "Kama Sutra" and "Ananga Ranga", and to Latin for his "Priapeia" and "Catullus"."

Foremost 16th century erotic writer

Pietro Aretino has been termed the "greatest erotic writer in Christendom." Perhaps his most famous work is the "Ragionamenti", partly biographical. Aretino was active as a writer for more than forty years, during which time he produced poetry and pornography, plays and theological works, lives of the saints and lampoons on the living. He was a friend of Michelangelo and Titian. He talked with popes. He has been depicted as "the Renaissance counterpart of Petronius in the ancient world, or of the Marquis de Sade in the period of European revolution."

Most famous French erotic novel apart from de Sade

The most famous erotic novel in the French language, apart from those of the Marquis, is "Gamiani", attributed to Alfred de Musset. This book, hardly heard of in modern England, went through forty-one editions before 1930. In one preface it is claimed that the author wrote it to prove that an erotic novel could be written without resort to "coarse" words. The theme in "Gamiani" – the title is from the surname of the heroine – is largely lesbian. A young man inadvertently witnesses a lesbian scene, whereupon he comes out of the cupboard and joins in. Most of the book is occupied with the ensuing love-triangle. One scene has Gamiani climbing onto the erection of a just hanged man. The plot ends with the two lesbians taking poison and experiencing orgasm and death simultaneously. A happy tale.

Most famous erotic novel

"Fanny Hill" wins this one hands down. Henry Cleland's "Fanny Hill or Memoirs of a Woman of Pleasure" was first published in London in 1749. The author sold it for twenty guineas to a bookseller, who is said to have made £10,000 from it. The book was quickly translated into several European languages. The style of the book is simple and artless, and "obscene" words are avoided by means of circumlocution and euphemism. The theme is straightforward to the point of cliché: a young innocent girl journeys to the big city and finds herself in a brothel, whereupon she quickly falls in love with one of the clients. The book ends with a happy marriage. "Fanny Hill" has been represented as the first truly erotic novel, and as providing useful insights into brothel-life in eighteenth-century London. Like all similar famous books of the genre, it has been prosecuted and praised.

First erotic book in Christian Europe

According to one authority, the first book of purely or mainly erotic content to be published in Christian Europe was the "Hermaphrodite" of Antonio Beccadelli, written in 1426. The Latin text was re-issued in 1892 with a French translation by Isidore Liseux, the scholarly French publisher of erotica and the literature of love. Beccadelli, who wrote under the name of Panormita, was one of the group of men later called humanist; he modelled much of his work on the writings of the poets of antiquity. Wayland Young suggests that Beccadelli, like Martial, was half fascinated and half disgusted "by women and fucking."

Most uninhibited sexual autobiography

"My Secret Life" by "Walter" is the most candid sexual autobiography in existence. For a start there are no diversions: the

work is all sex. In Casanova's "Memoirs" there are many asides, about gambling or magic or some such; and Frank Harris has given us a travelogue as well as an account of personal sexual experience. The 4000-odd pages of "My Secret Life" deal with nothing other than the sexual activities, enjoyments, frustrations, and insights of the author, in this sense the work is unique.

Most expensive sexual autobiography
Walter deserves another superlative! The full eleven volumes of "My Secret Life" are extremely rare, a real collector's item. What the work would cost today, if it were available is anybody's guess, but a copy is supposed to have been sold in 1926 for no less than seven thousand dollars.

FASHION
First brassieres
It all depends what you mean ... In various parts of ancient Greece the brassiere, in one form or other, was employed; paradoxically, in view of the free attitudes towards mixed nudity, naked athletics and the like, brassieres have been associated with the ancient inhabitants of Sparta. They were also used in China and elsewhere. The now almost extinct ancient Chinese brassiere has been likened to a small apron, introduced by Yang Kwei-fei, a concubine of Emperor Hsuan Tsung of T'amg in the eighth century. In fact the charming creature only decided on the creation of a "brassiere" to cover bites made by an "illegitimate" lover.

First topless dresses
The topless dress fashion of a few years ago may have seemed like a new thing. It wasn't. In fact an early purpose of the corset was to show as much of the breast as possible. As early as 1388, Johann de Mussi, a Lombard author, wrote – "Women show their breasts and it looks as if their breasts would wish to jump from their bosom". And he adds, reflectively, "Which gown would be beautiful if it did not show the breasts?" The beautiful Agnes Sorel (1409–1450) was said to display her shoulders and breasts, including the nipples. The early Christian Church term-

Nothing new in topless fashion. From the 1920's, a young girl in décolletage.

ed the laced openings to women's bodices "the gates of hell". By the fifteenth century much of the breast was again being shown; and in James I's time young unmarried women displayed the whole of their breasts. John Hill, a sixteenth-century poet comments "That women theyr breastes dyd shew & lay out." But the early Anglo-Saxons were predated by centuries in the use of topless fashions. In various mediterranean lands of antiquity the exposed breast was a commonplace. **63**

ART
Earliest depicted human coital positions

According to L. Legrain in "Ur Excavations, Vol. III: Archaic Seal Impressions" (1936), the oldest known depiction of human coitus, in the Ur excavations in Mesopotamia, dates to between 3200 and 3000 B.C. But much older than this are the representations of coital activity on the walls of the Grotte des Combarelles in the Dordogne in France. One particular drawing is thought to date from the Aurignacian period of the late Old Stone Age, about 40,000. If there are more ancient depictions than this we do not know of them.

What do we know of the first positions shown for coital activity? In the most ancient drawing, the one in the Dordogne, the woman is shown crouching forward while the man approaches her from behind. According to Havelock Ellis the oldest picture of human coitus that we have – of the Palaeolithic Solutrian age – shows the man as supine while the woman squats (in fact the Solutrian, or Solutrean age, ante-dates the Aurignacian). One prehistoric rock drawing, this time from Bohusian in Sweden, shows two couples standing up and copulating. And the seals from Ur of the Chaldees (around 3000 B.C.) have the copulating pair with the woman on top of the man. Kinsey et al have pointed out that the position with the woman above is common in ancient art, e.g. that of Peru, India, China, Japan and other civilizations. Perhaps the most famous of all the palaeolithic sexual depictions are those to be found in the Les Trois Frères cavern: a human figure, wearing an animal skin and antlers, is crouching, his genitals clearly shown (this drawing has often been cited as evidence of early witchcraft). Elsewhere in Trois Frères is an ithyphallic bison with human legs. And half-human, half-animal depictions are shown to suggest sexual mounting. A bone engraving from the Abri Murat (Lot) is based on the same theme. And in Pech Merle there is a finger drawing in clay of a woman "crouched in a sexually receptive posture beneath animal-like lines". (See P. Rawson, "Primitive Erotic Art").

The Venus of Laussel, pictured right, was originally carved on a rock shelter well over ten thousand
years ago.

Oldest Chinese sexual symbols

According to some authorities the most ancient Chinese representations of sexual subject matter date from the Tan dynasty (ca. 206 B.C.-A.D. 24) – "Excavations from that period have unearthed bricks from tombs and gifts buried with the dead which show definite sexual motifs." In view of the great antiquity of other aspects of Chinese erotic life these sexual motifs do not seem particularly ancient. The sexual manuals in China suggest that various forms of sexual imagery would have been employed two or three thousand years before the birth of Christ.

Earliest female nude sculpture

The prehistoric sculptures such as the Venus of Willendorf are among the oldest to show the nude female figure. Such works are generally dated to palaeolithic times. The relief carvings such as the Venus of Laussel may also be mentioned (See Edward Lucie-Smith, "Eroticism in Western Art"). Originally deriving from a rock shelter, it is now in a museum at Bordeaux. The figure (about 46 cm tall) was originally carved on a block overhanging a sanctuary, and is probably Solutrian in date. She had been coloured red to

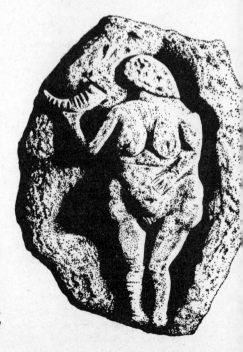

signify power and life; and her breasts, belly, hips and thighs bulge with fat. Her hand rests on his stomach, and the pubic triangle is emphasized. Her attributes are clearly sexual. There has been speculation about the relation of the figure with animal fertility cults. What is particularly interesting about these early representations is that they are not naturalistic, in the way that the early paintings of animals are naturalistic. Instead certain sexual features are exaggerated, such as the thighs and breasts. The apparent desirability of fatness, common also to primitive societies in the modern world, has been attributed to the survival value of stored body food. In the late Stone Age an Aurignacian sculptor created what has come to be known as the Venus of Lespugue, a palaeolithic female figure carved in the ivory of the mammoth's tusk found in the Haute-Garonne in 1922 (See G. S. Whittet, "Lovers in Art"). The period runs from about 30,000 B.C. to 10,000 B.C.

Most famous ancient nude sculpture

The Cnidian Aphrodite (or Venus) of Praxiteles is generally said to be the most famous statue in the ancient world. It has been dated to the fourth century B.C., and the work was seemingly known throughout many of the lands of antiquity. In the tenth century the work, having been taken to Constantinople by Theodosius, was praised by the Emperor Constantine Porphyrogenitus; and the statue, in original or copy, is mentioned by Robert de Clari in his account of the taking of Constantinople by the Crusaders.

The Cnidian Venus after Praxiteles

Most famous erotic sculpture

The most famous erotic sculpture in the world is certainly that of the Hindu temples of India (See P. Rawson, "Erotic Art of the East"). Most of the best examples were created in the North between the ninth and thirteen centuries A.D., and in the South between the sixth and seventeenth centuries A.D. The sculptures show every imaginable form of sexual activity – different coital positions, oral sex, masturbation, rape, bestiality, etc.

Many temples still used for worship make use of immense wooden-wheeled chariots or "cars," constructed after the pattern of the temples, with high canopies and spires. The chariots are used to carry the sacred images during the festivals, and they are adorned with the same sorts of erotic scenes as are the temples themselves. The carvings, elaborate and meticuolusly executed, show all forms of sexual behaviour.

Largest organs displayed in erotic art

Some erotic art, notably that of Japan, is characterized by immense exaggeration of the sexual organs. The penis and vulva are often drawn three or four times their proper size: the penis, for example, can resemble a forearm, and the female organ often "assumes the length and width of the folded sleeve opening of a kimono". One extraordinary feature of Japanese erotic art is the depiction of the penis as a duelling weapon. Drawings show two men, both equipped with mighty organs, fencing with the erect members. There are also other forms of penis competitions: men are depicted going along to have vast organs measured to see who possesses the largest. In one drawing a man equipped with a penis about the size of all the rest of him is obliged to support the mighty organ on a pair of wagonwheels trundling before him! A sexual hero of China was said to be able to smash a copper pot with one blow of his penis!

Earliest sexual designs were used for porcelain by the Manchu emperors.

First Chinese erotic porcelain

Sexual designs were used for porcelain ware by the Manchu emperors such as Ch'ien Lung and Hsien Feng, as a form of sexual elaboration. Erotic motifs and designs were used on vases, bowls, plates, etc.; it has been established that such designs were painted on earthenware in the first and third centuries. One early Chinese habit was to bury earthen bowls and plates where "future rebel leaders or rulers might be born." It was thought that earthenware carrying erotic designs would bring ill luck to future rulers and thus forestall possible uprisings.

First Chinese erotic jade and ivory

Erotic carvings gradually appeared in Chinese jade and ivory. An eye-witness in the Ming Dynasty described such things from the Ming Palace "The two Happy Buddhas were carved out of two huge pieces of flawless jade. With their sex organs in close contact they gave the viewers the basic concept of the man-woman relationship. The eunuch in charge told me that these jade figures were actually left behind in the palace by the Mongols after their downfall. He also said that they had been used by the Mongol imperial family to enlighten their descendants about the facts of life. It is believed that after our empire had been established, these figures continued to be used for the same purpose during the reign of our first few emperors. However, I cannot help congratulating myself secretly for having the good luck to see these finished products of artistic perfection."

67

First erotic coins

China also boasted erotic coins ("spring coins") as early as the Han Dynasty. On one side of a coin would be words of good omen; on the other, a god and a goddess would be copulating. It was claimed that such coins could dispel evil spirits, as a consequence of which, parents frequently gave them to their children as a form of protection against supernatural forces. By the time of the Sung Dynasty the coins were showing a variety of coital positions: they were no longer called "spring coins" but "bed-curtain-spreading coins." They formed an integral part of a dowry when a daughter married; on the wedding-night the coins would be scattered on the bridal bed. In other cultures with a strong erotic tradition and a coinage system coins were also used to depict sexual activity. For example, in pre-Christian Greece some coins show an eager satyr carrying off a complaisant nymph (mid-sixth century B.C.). And there is a Greek scaraboid of the fifth century B.C., showing a cock treading a hen; an identical scene appears on an Etruscan gem of the same period.

Greatest Chinese erotic painter

Chou Fang is regarded as the greatest Chinese erotic painter. Mi Fei, a famous painter in the Sung Dynasty, held Chou in the same class as Ku Kai-chih (one of whose pictures is in the British Museum), Lu T'ang-wei, and Wu Tao-tzu. The women in Chou's paintings are all rather plump – which relates to the T'ang Dynasty concept of beauty. Chou Fang, in common with many oriental artists, also tended to exaggerate the size of the genital organs: it is said that he influenced Japanese erotic art.

Peak period of Japanese erotic art

Japanese erotic art is generally regarded as reaching a peak during the Edo period, 1600–1868; Edo refers to the small fishing

Above: Ming dynasty Chinese jade. Below: from the Edo period of Japanese art by Harunobu and, left, by Koryusai.

town which was to succeed the old city of Kyoto as capital of Japan and which was to become the Tokyo of today. The Edo period saw a quite unparalleled development of erotic art and literature, one consequence of which was that the Japanese government started to take an interest in censorship!

Above: Giorgione's "The Dresden Venus" Right: Titian's "Venus of Urbino"

First reclining nude in European erotic art

It is thought that Giorgione and Titian were the first painters to use a reclining nude woman as the subject of a painting. Where, before their time, such a position occurs, as on some Roman sarcophagi, the figure is only a detail, filling in the corners to complete the design. The use of the nude woman in such a way was secondary to the main design. Giorgione and Titian in both sculpture and painting elevated the reclining nude to a significant status, and this is the teeth of opposition from the Christian Church to all things carnal.

Most famous Spanish love painting

The most famous of the few Spanish love-paintings is the fairy-tale "St George and the Dragon" (c. 1438, Art Institute of Chicago) by Bernat Martorel. The style is linked in its conventions to the illumination of manuscripts. The original Saint George is thought to have died about A.D. 300 at Lydda in Palestine. He seemingly assumed his role of a slayer of dragons from Perseus who slew a sea monster that had threatened the virgin Andromeda. The ideals of courtly love "were exalted to the sanctification of the perfect, gentle knight."

First Renaissance nude sculpture

There are nudes and nudes. Some are desiccated and sexless, others jaunty and provocative. According to one authority (E. Carr, "European Erotic Art"), the first nude of the Renaissance – a nude that is "not unaesthetic and submissive, the usual appearance of the Byzantine and medieval Eves" – is Lorenzo Ghiberti's *Eve* on the eastern door of the Baptistry in Florence, sculptured in relief in 1425. She is given the Hebrew name of Eve and she is being called into existence by Jehovah, but she has the beautiful expression reminiscent of the Greek Venus on the Ludovisi throne and the body is "unashamedly beautiful..." (Ghiberti also wrote the earliest known autobiography of an artist.)

First Italian Renaissance painter of erotic art

Antonio Pisanello (c. 1395–c. 1455) has been taken as one of the first Italian artists to see in the nude form the wide scope for erotic art. He produced copies of the Bacchic Sarcophagi in the Campo Santo collection of antique art in Pisa, and then added to some of these an erotic component; for instance he drew the legs of a young girl to suggest "uninhibited delight in sexuality."

Earliest pornographic artist in England

The earliest pornographic artist in England, with name unknown, functioned halfway through the eighteenth-century. In about 1755 he produced seventeen drawings to illustrate "The Pleasures of Love: Containing a Variety of Entertaining Particulars and Curiosities in the Cabinet of Venus." The frontispiece shows a fat woman, with a basin of cordial in her left hand, the right drawing aside the curtains of a bed on which can be seen four naked legs. On the curtain is inscribed "The pleasures of Love 1755." The book was reprinted in 1881 as "The Adventures of a Rake," and in reprint the book carried inferior illustrations.

"That's all I ever hear: 'just one more sitting'!"

GRAFFITI
Most frequent sexual references by females

Graffiti, as we all know, is not always sexual in nature. It is more often sexual when produced by men than when produced by women. Kinsey and his colleagues investigated sexual and non-sexual graffiti (as they appear to have investigated everything else) and documented and tabulated their results. A high proportion (86 per cent) of the inscriptions on the walls of the male toilets were found to be sexual; but not more than 25 per cent of the toilet wall inscriptions made by women dealt with sexual topics (genitals, oral and anal sexual behaviour, "obscene" words, etc.). Most of the female inscriptions referred to love, or names were associated ("John and Mary," "Helen and Don"); the drawing of hearts was common in the female toilets. In 331 female inscriptions, there were 69 per cent depicting lips, 35 per cent making non-erotic references to love with the opposite sex, and 12 per cent making non-erotic references to love with own sex. The scores in the other Kinsey categories were considerably less.

This anonymous inscriber lays claim to sexual graffiti as one branch of erotic art.

Least frequent sexual references by females

Surprisingly, amongst the 331 female in-scriptions there were no references to heterosexual dating (homosexual dating scored one per cent). There were no homosexual references to anal contacts, and only one per cent heterosexual reference to anal activity. Oral contacts scores two per cent (heterosexual) and one per cent (homosexual); "other erotic items" also scored two per cent (both heterosexual and homosexual).

Most frequent sexual references by males

The investigators found 1048 sexual and non-sexual inscriptions in male toilets, of which the largest category (30 per cent) were homosexual oral contacts, with heterosexual oral contacts scoring only eleven per cent. Twenty-one per cent of the inscriptions were to homosexual dating and eighteen per cent to homosexual anal contacts.

Least frequent references by men

The least frequent references by men were to "non-erotic" items such as lips and hearts (none recorded). Three per cent of inscriptions related to the genitalia of the opposite sex; and non-erotic references to love (both with the same and the opposite sex) also scored three per cent. Five per cent of the inscriptions referred to heterosexual dating.

POETRY
Most important poet in Rome

This is Catullus, the first Roman love-poet. He has been considered "more sympathetic to modern minds than all his famous successors; for he is a man, not a rhetorician, and he tells us frankly and beautifully of his passion." Catullus has been seen as bisexual, with the heterosexual side of his nature predominating. Inevitably he has been portrayed as a coarse and pornographic writer.

Most famous "kissing" poet

Robert Herrick has been dubbed the "Kissing Poet." For instance his "Hesperides", 1648, is replete with kisses and kissing. In Catullus there is a kissing poem. Herrick has his own version –

Tempora cinxiss et Foliorum densior umbra:
Debetur Genio Laurea Sylva tuo.
Tempora et Illa Tibi mollis redimisset Oliva,
Scilicet excludis Versibus Arma tuis.
Admisces Antiqua Novis, Jucunda Severis:
Hinc Juvenis discat, Fæmina Virgo Senex,
Ut solo minor es Phœbo, sic major es Unus
Omnibus, Ingenio Mente, Lepore, Stylo.
scripsit I.H.C.W.M.

*Ah my Anthea! Must my heart still
    break?
(Love makes me write, what shame
    forbids to speak.)
Give me a kisse, adde to that kisse a
    score;
Then to that twenty, adde an hundred
    more;
A thousand to that thousand; so kisse
    on,
To make that thousand up a million.
Treble that million, and when that is
    done,
Let's kisse afresh, as when we first
    begun.
But yet, though Love likes well such
    Scenes as these,
There is an act that will more fully
    please:
Kissing and glancing, soothing, all make
    way
But to the acting of this private play:
Name it I would; but being blushing
    red,
The rest Ile speak, when we meet both
    in bed.*

Greatest European sexual-love poet

This superlative, like many of the others, is a matter of opinion. But for this one a fair number of people seem to opt for Racine. Racine has been represented as seeing love as a passion – "that is, something suffered by mankind, a thing imposed upon mankind from outside – and ultimately, therefore, an ill."

Most famous sensual poem
If the Song of Solomon is a poem then it qualifies for this one. In the nineteenth century the Reverend E. P. Eddrupp, Prebendary of Salisbury Cathedral wrote in a commentary on the Old Testament – "Such a book as the Song of Solomon may not be fitted for public reading in a mixed congregation, or even for private reading by the impure in heart." The first-century Pharisees wondered whether the Song should have a place in the Canon: the problem was that the Song so clearly celebrates physical (or carnal) love and makes no reference to God. Inevitably there were endless attempts to interpret the Song metaphorically or allegorically. It is supposed to have been written about 400 B.C., during the reign of Artaxerxes II.

Foremost 14th century lyricist
Guillaume de Machaut, born in Champagne around the year 1300, was the dominant figure both in lyric poetry and music in fourteenth-century France. Many of his own poems were specifically arranged for musical setting. In a famous work combining both poetry and music, Le Livre du Voir Dit, probably written between 1361 and 1365, Machaut recounts the progress of his love affair with a young girl called Péronne. At this time the poet was more than sixty years old and blind in one eye. It is likely that the girl was more impressed by the man's reputation as a poet and composer than by the amorous possibilities of the situation. Machaut is considered one of the central figures in the art of courtly love.

First clandestine production of an erotic work
In 1674 an effort was made at All Souls College, Oxford, using the university press, to prepare an edition of Aretino's

"Sonnets", illustrated by Romano's celebrated drawings of coital positions. Alas, it so happened that the Dean appeared unexpectedly – with no less than sixty reproductions already produced. Consideration was given to the possibility of expulsion – "And I think they would deserve it, were they of any other college than All Souls, but there I will allow them to be virtuous that are bawdy only in pictures."

First erotic writer in English

This is a debatable one. Atkins plumps for Spenser as "the first writer in English to be consciously erotic." The "Faerie Queen" is represented as a "mine of sensuality." A "Spectator" article is cited to indicate the sexual significance of the Spenser imagery – "You do not need any psychoanalytic training to see here a rather grisly amalgam of the male and female sexual organs," after quoting the description of the lustful monster in Book IV, Canto VII. Now it's Atkins again – Spenser reckoned to be preaching chastity and religion, but he "allowed his imagination to luxuriate in obscenities which would have impressed both Shakespeare and Donne."

"Watch out, Samuel Pepys"

PUBLICATIONS
First erotic periodical in U.K.

This emerged in 1773, under the title "The Covent Garden Magazine," *Amorous Repository, Calculated Solely for the Entertainment of the Polite World*. In the words of Hurwood, "This, inauspicious as it may have seemed at the time, the great granddaddy of a multi-million dollar business was born." Ten years later London acquired a new publication – "The Rambler's Magazine": Or, *The Annals of Gallantry, Glee, Pleasure, and the Bon Ton; Calculated for the entertainment of the Polite World; and to furnish the Man of Pleasure with a most delicious banquet of Amorous, Bacchanalian, Whimsical, Humorous Theatrical, and Polite Entertainment*. As a principal item readers were offered the histories of ladies "whom the attracing charms of gold can conquer," and typical story titles were *The History and Adventure of a Bedstead, The Adventures of a Eunuch, Memoirs of Lydia Lovemore*, and the *Adventures of Kitty Pry*.

Most famous 19th century porno magazine

It is difficult to say what the difference is between erotica and pornography. Those who praise sexual manifestations in art will tend to use the former word, those who are perpetually disgusted by all things carnal will incline to savour the latter. To say of a magazine that it was "pornographic" is not necessarily to condemn it, nor, *mutatis mutandis*, is it to praise it. However, one publication popularly dubbed *pornographic* in the nineteenth century was "The Pearl" – which carried the happy subtitle, *Journal of Facetiae and Voluptuous Reading*. The journal appeared monthly between July 1879 and December 1886, and declared as its imprint, Oxford: Printed at the University Press. The entire run, in three volumes, contained 36 obscene coloured lithographs – said by Ashbee to be of "vile execution." Six serialized novels were also included, as well as short stories, numerous ballads, poems, "gossip" notes and anecdotes, amounting to a total of five hundred pages. Some items, in translation, were simply stolen from elsewhere. "The Pearl" was neither the first nor the last of its kind; it was the most famous.

First girlie mags

The first "girlie magazines" were intended to be *respectable*, emphatically not "pornographic". The first magazine to merit the adjective "girlie" was "Esquire", which, in the 1930s, was the only one of its kind. The decision to carry pin-ups was bold and innovative; "Esquire" began, incidentally, as a men's fashion magazine, hence the status title. The first issue of the magazine had a printing of 105,000 copies, 5,000 of which were to be distributed to newsstands and 100,000 to clothing stores throughout the U.S. The first issue was, however, so popular that 95,000 copies were recalled from clothiers and redistributed to newsstands. The first issue was also significant in that it carried George Petty's famous pin-up girl, appearing at first more as a cartoon than a pin-up. She soon represented a singular female type that was destined to become almost as much a legend as the Gibson girl had been thirty years earlier. In early 1941, the Petty girls began to appear regularly in "Esquire's" first foldout pages.

First magazine exposure of pubic hair

The first exposure of pubic hair – "albeit modest to the point of invisibility" was accomplished by "Penthouse" (April 1970). The appearance of pubic hair in the girlies is now so commonplace that it is remarkable that there was such a fuss about it in 1970. But at the time the "Penthouse" initiative was seen as little short of revolutionary! Almost all the other "pin-up" magazines followed suit within a matter of months.

First erotic magazine for women

It is a commonplace of sexological research that women are supposed to be less easily aroused by visual erotica than are men: this is found in the bulk of relevant research from Kinsey onwards, but some of the findings are ambiguous. Recently various women have been involved in the creation of "pin-up" magazines for women. The two most famous of such magazines are "Viva" and "Playgirl". Are women, suddenly confronted with a graphic centrespread penis fastened onto a handsome male, stimulated to lustful urges? I don't know. The only girl I asked

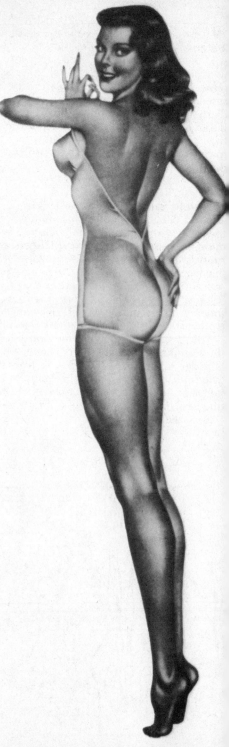

The painting illustrated above is by Varga and depicts "Miss January, Nineteen Forty-Six!" in "Esquire" magazine.

declared that it didn't do much for her – but she kept looking!

Most famous 19th century female erotica publisher

Perhaps the most famous woman publisher of erotica in the nineteenth-century was Mary Wilson. Whether she published primarily for men or for women is not known, but she produced a wide variety of literature. She was called by the famous "governess," Theresa Berkeley, "the reviver of erotic literature in the present century." Mary Wilson had a number of peculiarities, one of which was an intense dislike of sodomy in any form; she would allow no mention of it to appear in any of her books. She also wrote an essay in a collection called "The Voluptuarian Cabinet"; the piece was called *Adultery on the Part of Married Women, and Fornication on the Part of Old Maids and Widows defended by Mary Wilson, Spinster, With Plans for Promoting the same, Addressed to the Ladies of the Metropolis and its Environs*. The plan was for the establishment of a palatial brother for women only. It was to be a sanctuary "to which any lady of rank and fortune may subscribe, and to which she may repair incog; the married to commit what the world calls adultery, and the single to commit what at the tabernacle is termed fornication, or in a gentler phrase, to obey the dictates of all powerful Nature, by offering up a cheerful sacrifice to the God Priapus, the most ancient of deities." The plan, alas, never materialized.

Most famous 20th century erotica publisher

The most famous modern dynasty in the publishing of erotica is centered in Paris. Before the war an Anglo-Irishman named Jack Kahane founded the Obelisk Press and published Joyce's "Haveth Childers" (a foretaste of "Finnegan's Wake"), Durrell's "The Black Book", Conolly's "The Rock Pool," and Harris's "Life and Loves". His son, Maurice Girodias, continued the family business and has published Nabokov's "Lolita", Donleavy's "The Ginger bread Man" and Burrough's "The Naked Lunch". The firm now publishes as Olympia Press. In 1972

"Scorpio" ran an article, "Is Maurice Girodias Being Forced Out of Pornography?", indicating the immense difficulties under which he was operating. At the same time there appears to be an increasing willingness to admit that Girodias has made a significant and enduring contribution to modern literature. After all he was even asked to contribute a piece to "To Deprave and Corrupt ...," a compilation including items from such respectable people as Lord Birkett and Norman St. John-Stevas.

Most unexpected appearance of "fuck" in print

In some circumstances the word *fuck* is used where we more or less expect it – in pornography, modern novels, and "progressive" talk. Historically it has sometimes appeared when least expected: for instance the dread word slipped into the columns of "The Times" (London) on 13 January 1882. The report of a speech delivered by the Attorney General, Sir William Harcourt, included one man's sentiment that "he felt like a bit of fucking." The shock at this in Printing House Square was so great that a full four days elapsed before "the management of this journal" could steel itself to issue an apology – it spoke of "gross outrage," of a "malicious fabrication" that was "surreptitiously introduced" and noted that the matter was under legal investigation – "it is to be hoped that the perpetrator of the outrage will be brought to punishment." "The Times" suffered another terrible blow when an advertisement for a book about the public schools was discovered, after the paper had been printed, to include the line – "With a Glossary of Some Words used by Henry Irving in his disquisitions upon fucking, which is in common use in these schools." And this only a few months after the first incident! Not a good year for "The Times". It is also noted that in a daily paper reporting the birth of a royal child – "the substitution of an F for a B in the name of the palace where the queen was confined gave the heading of the notice a suspiciously suggestive appearance." All in all, Kenneth Tynan's delivery of the word *fuck* on BBC television had one or two "establishment" precedents.

Most successful erotica promoter in U.K.

Paul Raymond, born Geoffrey Anthony Quinn, the son of a Liverpool haulage contractor, is without doubt the most successful individual promoter of magazine and theatrical erotica in Britain today. His "Men Only" is one of the best-selling girlie magazines in Britain, with "Club International", from the same Fleet Street stable, also chalking up impressive sales. In addition he now has five London theatres, including the Revuebar, the Windmill, and the Whitehall (this latter is said to have cost him £340,000). His most expensive show – costing around £300,000 to stage – was the "Royalty Follies"; the £25,000 production costs of "Pyjama Tops" at the Whitehall were recouped in just two months. Paul Raymond – one-time drummer, salesman, barman, and miner – claims he could have sold the Revuebar for £1.25 million. One Raymond quote – "Tits, bums and a few laughs. That's what people like. That's what I like. I'm not a pornographer, I'm an entertainer. And I have a knack of judging what people want at any given moment."

Left: Paul Raymond, foremost UK erotica promoter, "I have a knack of judging what people want."

There was never anything seedy about the Follies. Above, a classic pose from a pre-war production.

A pre-war production of the Folies Bergère at the London Palladium.

"It's magnificent, but is it ballet?"

THEATRE
Most famous nun playwright
The tenth-century German nun Hrot-
switha wrote, in Latin, a remarkable series
of plays strongly influenced by the pagan
Roman dramatist Terence (c. 190-159 B.C.).
But she manages to be sexier! In fact some
of her scenes are set in brothels. One
represents a cemetery where a lover inter-
rogates a sexton. The intruder wants to dig
up his mistress's corpse. Go ahead, says the
sexton, she's not putrid yet. You'll find her
still in fair condition for fornication. Ha,
cries the lover, as he seizes a spade, Now I
can offer that bitch all the insults I please!
(Abutere, ut licet – Nunc in mea situm est
potestate quantislibet iniuriis te velim
lacessere.)

First appearance of actresses in
Shakespearean play
The appearance of women on the stage
82 got under way in earnest when Tom

Killigrew, one of the King's best friends,
produced "Othello" on 8 December
1660. Women had already appeared in
plays on the Continent. In England no self-
respecting young woman would have
thought of a career in acting – and so all
the casting was done in brothels! The
subject-matter of plays being performed
was such that whores fitted naturally into
the female roles. Theatre thrived on love
intrigues, rape, seduction, and the like. It
has been said that Restoration theatre "not
only fostered lewdness by depicting it in
glowing and attractive colours, but its
actors spread abroad the corruption it was
their business to delineate" – "Their
personal character corresponded, in too
many instances, with the parts which they
performed, and they re-enacted in private
the debaucheries which they presented on
the stage."

*A woman first appeared nude on stage at the
Folies-Bergère in Paris in 1912.*

First nude woman on stage

The first time that a woman appeared on the stage completely nude was at the Folies-Bergère in 1912. She was only visible for a moment. It was feared that a scandal would follow but France survived, and after the war every Paris revue featured at least one naked woman.

First presentation of lesbianism

The first major effort to present lesbianism on the American stage was suppressed by the police. This was in 1927, and the play was the French importation, "The Captive," by Edouard Bourdet. The play was devoid of any message. It concerned a love triangle, two women and a man. One of the women, inevitably enough, did not know to which of the others to turn. This, evidently, was too strong for the authorities of the day!

Intimations of auto-eroticism in the first recorded instance of sex in advertising. A woodcut published in Belgium in 1491.

ADVERTISING
First instance of sex

In one view, Eve tempting Adam is the first case of sex in advertising, though perhaps this is not normally what we think of by the phrase. Another candidate for the title is a woodcut produced in 1491 by a Belgian publisher to promote a new translation of "Histoire de la Belle Melusine" by Jean d'Arras. The woodcut may be regarded as the first known illustrated advertising poster. Melusine's breasts are exposed (she is bathing), and there is some suggestion of auto-eroticism in the position of her right hand. The text beneath the illustration reads – "A beautiful, pleasing, and most marvellous story of a lady named Melusine, of her ancestors and descendants, and the wonderful and devout works and deeds they wrought and performed. Lately translated from the French into Flemish and adorned with fine personages and scenes as the text demands. This story, as well as a great number of other new books, can be purchased at the price written hereunder."

Most famous sexy "double entendre"

Elliott White Springs, in 1947, shocked the business community in the U.S. with his double entendre concerning the Spring-maid name. Making use of sex appeal to sell sheets, Springs – a pioneer of quarter of a century ago – used a cartoon of an Indian couple on a sheet hammock. The caption read – "A buck well spent on a Springmaid sheet."

PHOTOGRAPHY

Earliest bathing beauty postcard

The earliest postcards of bathing beauties came from France around 1900, and soon after that such cards were made available in England. The first bathing scenes were created by artists. Later, when a camera was used the model was usually posed against a hand-drawn beach background. Postcards in the early 1900s featured "French Actresses," "Japanese Beauties" dressed in traditional costume, "Actresses" in colour, and ballet dancers and bathers posing in tights. Some card manufacturers glued silk, oilcloth, or spangles on their pin-up cards.

Above: Lautrec's "Debauche" Below: early postcard.

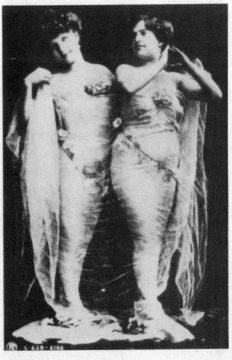

First nude calendar

In 1913, the first-known calendar nude appeared, called "September Morn", a reproduction of an oil painting, "Matinée Septembre", by a French artist, Paul Chabas (1869-1937). The painting might have gone unnoticed if Comstock, of the Society for the Suppression of Vice, had not demanded the removal of the painting from the window of a New York art gallery. A salesman explained that the painting had recently won a Medal of Honour from the French Academy, but we may presume, Comstock was not impressed.

First girlie calendar

Brown and Bigelow of Saint Paul, Minnesota, is the world's oldest calendar company. Around 1903 the firm produced its first calendar with a female subject – "Colette" (from a painting from Angelo Asti), a "charming but conservative portrait of a young beauty." In the years that followed, "Colette" helped to sell more than 1.5 million calendars. In 1904 the first pin-up calendar indicated that the manufacture of "girlie" calendars could be a lucrative business.

First nude photographer

It has been claimed that the French photographer Lerebours photographed some nudes as early as 1840, only one year after the historic introduction of Daguerre's process (P. Lacey, "The History of the Nude in Photography"). It was suggested that the interest in the nude at this period was not only aesthetic – professional models were among the first live subjects capable of holding a pose for the required five to ten minutes. The Parisian photographers, Nadar and Durieu, were among the first in the world to photograph nudes.

First nude photography magazine

The first nude photography magazine was "Camera Work", founded in 1902 by Alfred Stieglitz. Not all the pictures were of nudes, but nude photographs were frequent, usually in portfolios by such photographers as Annie Brigman, Clarence Whitehead, Robert Demarchy, Renée Le Begue and Frank Eugene. The treatment was such as to suggest "feelings and associations beyond the actual subject." In particular, "Camera Work" included studies by the Photo-Secessionists.

First female pin-up

In 1887, Charles Dana Gibson – then twenty years of age – began a long-term contract with "Life". As a young man, Gibson "dipped his pen in the cosmic urge and tried to draw a girl so alluring that other young men would want to climb into the picture and sit beside her." By the time of the 1890s the Gibson girl was well established, and she was a front-runner for twenty years. In 1903, Gibson signed a hundred thousand dollar contract with "Collier's" (1886-1957) to render a series of double-page "cartoons" over four years' time. "The Gibson Girl was not simply a model but represented a way of life."

First U.K. male pin-up

Paul de Feu, reclining in a suitably modest position, was photographed nude for a full-colour, double-page spread in "Cosmopolitan" (London), April 1972. It was of some interest that Mr. de Feu, aged 36, was married to, but separated from, Germaine Greer, the keen champion of Women's Lib. A construction worker and college graduate, Mr. de Feu described his posing as "striking a blow for male servitude." He was quoted in "Time" (14/2/72) as saying

"I'm a guy who likes birds. Normally I'd spend a lot of time, chat, and money taking a girl out in the hopes of getting somewhere with her. This way – being a pin-up – I've got to the clothes-off stage with thousands of birds straightaway." During the same month "Cosmopolitan" (New York) printed a centrefold nude photograph of the American actor Burt Reynolds.

*Paul de Feu, construction worker, college graduate
and sometime husband of Germaine Greer
"striking a blow for male servitude".*

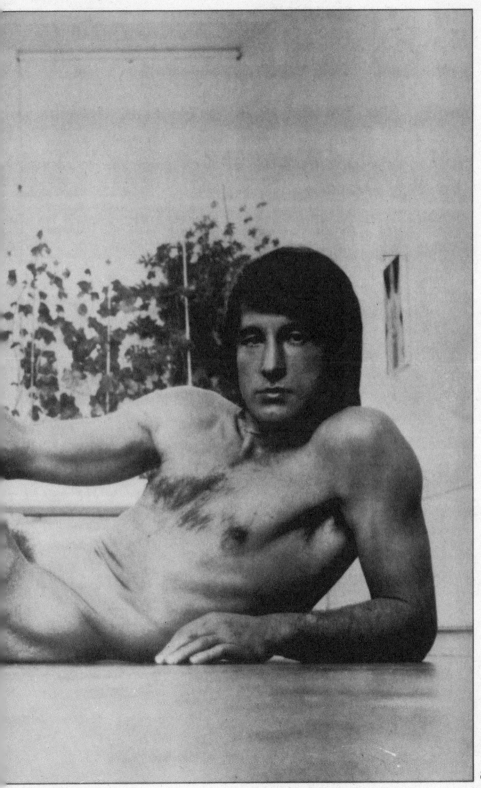

Most famous female nude photographer

There have been a number of distinguished female photographers of the nude in the twentieth century, including Emy Andriesse of Holland, and Nell Dorr and Ruth Bernhard of the United States. Miss Bernhard's work is the best known, having appeared regularly in magazines and books over the last three decades. She has been quoted as saying – "If I have chosen the female form in particular, it is because beauty has been debased and exploited in our sensual twentieth-century. We seem to have a need to turn innocent nature into evil ugliness by the twist of the mind. Woman has been the target of much that is sordid and cheap, especially in photography. To raise, to elevate, to endorse with timeless reverence the image of woman, has been my mission – the reason for my work which you see here."

First front page streaker photograph

Streaking – the 1974 fashion of running naked from one point to another – has been variously attributed to "dares" means of raising money for charity, simple exhibitionism, or the more complex motives beloved of psychiatrists. The press loved the streaking phenomenon since it proved an excuse, if any were needed, to supply pleasantly titillating copy and to print nude pictures. The "Daily Mirror" (18/3/74) had the happy distinction of being the first large-circulation newspaper internationally to show us an active streaker on its front page. An attractive blonde streaker called Sally is shown pinned against the wall by a London policeman.

PC221 and his boisterous dog corner Sally the streaker after a mad nude dash across Kingston Bridge over the Thames in London.

Woman: "the target of much that is sordid and cheap, especially in photography."

FILMS
First female sex symbol
Theda Bara was the first screen vamp. She was also the first star to have a screen personality specially created for her. Bara wore erotic costumes which often scarcely concealed her breasts or buttocks. "A couple of loosely spun spider's webs did duty for a bra, or else an asp curved snugly around the contours of each breast, while a few bead whorls appliquéd on her hip bone by gum arabic looked like some satyr's erotic doodling." She also had a liking for wearing metal chains against the naked flesh "in a way that carried an undertone of perversion". Theda Bara began her epic career before the First World War.

Oldest woman to become a sex symbol
Mae West has been portrayed as one of the very few stars who was "self-made and self-sustaining," owing her success to herself alone, not to a director, scriptwriter, make-up artist, or photographer. What is perhaps most remarkable about her is that she first arrived at Hollywood when she was forty years of age – "grotesquely late to begin a film career".

Theda Bara
Mae West

First star to use her breasts to arouse
The eroticism of Theda Bara was *generalized*, with no particular item or mode of behaviour coming in for particular emphasis. In any event her breasts were not vast, so there was little scope for concentration on them! Not so with Jean Harlow. This latter actress usually gets the credit for focussing the erotic interest, for the first time on the screen, on a woman's breasts. At the end of the nineteen-twenties it was the flat-chested flappers who symbolized screen sex. Harlow's breasts were only large (34-inch bust) compared to the boyish females who had appeared on the screen before her – but she heaved up her breasts and used them to advantage. Harlow was said to be a compulsive exhibitionist, a "sexual provocatrice who knew the effect her body made on men." Her nipples were supposed to expand as the room temperature went up; and before a Press conference she would rub them with ice.

Most famous sex symbol

This must be Marilyn Monroe, despite the current popularity of Bo Derek. Monroe featured on the most publicized calendar in history, published in 1951 by John Baumgarth Co. The original nude picture was taken in May 1949 by Tom Kelly, a California photographer. Kelly is supposed to have remarked at the time – "This wasn't just another girl. This was a girl with instinct for drama and showmanship. Her lips parted provocatively, her body was arched and magnificent. There was a natural grace about her." A series of later films made Monroe the leading American sex-symbol. Her mysterious death, following rumours of possible liaisons with eminent Americans, added something to her already vast legend. It was a simple matter to declare that she committed suicide. According to one report, however, no chemical "sludge" was found in her stomach after death. This has been held as evidence that she did not, in fact, commit suicide.

Marilyn Monroe
Jean Harlow

Brigitte Bardot

and "Blood and Sand" (1922). When he died in hospital in 1926, thousands of people stopped the traffic. In addition several women committed suicide, 100,000 condolence telegrams were sent, and a monument erected to his memory was set up in Hollywood.

Longest lasting male romantic lead

Cary Grant has been an immensely successful romantic lead in Hollywood for more than thirty years. No other male actor can compete with this record. One of his best known films – "Holiday" – appeared in 1938; yet still Cary Grant plays successful romantic leads.

Most famous European sex symbol

Brigitte Bardot enjoyed the reputation as the most famous European pin-up girl of the mid-twentieth-century. She had been depicted as "moodier, tougher, more independent, and adventurous than Marilyn Monroe..." Like Monroe she has had a checkered life in private and public. Bardot, however, has proved the more durable.

Most famous male film star lover

Rudolph Valentino began his career as a dancer, then rose to stardom as a dark passionate lover in "The Four Horsemen of the Apocalypse" (1921), "The Sheik,"

Most notorious U.S. censorship code

In 1921 the U.S. Motion Picture Producers and Distributors of America Inc. asked W. H. Hays, a prominent Republican, to be their president in an effort to ward of plans for government censorship. One of the first Hays initiatives was to insert a "morality clause" into all actors' contract forcing them to maintain at least a facade of clean living. In 1930 his Production Code was adopted by the industry; in 193- it was made mandatory, with fines and sanctions on any film-maker who ignored it. The Code had a statement of general aims followed by twelve sections of "Particular Applications." These latter inclu-

Rudolph Valentino

led such declarations as "The treatment of bedrooms must be governed by good taste and delicacy" and "Suicide, as a solution of problems occurring in the development of screen drama is to be discouraged as morally questionable." Inevitably, all sex organs – even those of children – were forbidden for screen representation, as were all forms of "perversion." The critic George Jean Nathan has commented that the effect of the Hays Office Code on Hollywood film-making was "to picture most characters in their amorous reactions to each other as practically indistinguishable from little children dressed up in their parents' clothes and playing house."

First breast exposure in modern times
In the silent film days there was nothing to a bit of breast exposure. It was a commonplace of epic and small-scale production alike. In modern times, after a lapse lasting a decade or two, the battle had to 95

Left: Linda Lovelace   *Above: W. H. Hayes*

be fought all over again, until the breast and other anatomical bits and pieces eventually won through! On 29 March 1965, a Negress in "The Pawnbroker", also starring Rod Steiger, exposed both her breasts to the full, thereby breaking Section Seven, Sub-section Two of the Motion Picture Production Role – "Indecent or undue exposure is forbidden." A commentator wrote – "For the first time in the history of the Hollywood Production Code, official recognition has been given to the good taste and artistic merit with which a subject is treated, not only to whether it hews to the current standards by which the Code is interpreted." A headline in "Variety" noted, more succinctly, "Film Part requires no Bra." "The Pawnbroker" later became the official United States entry in the 1964 Berlin Film Festival.

First exposure of pubic hair
This is another tricky one. Avid researchers into such matters have scrutinized films frame by frame. Was it hair or was it shadow? Not that it matters all that much, but some people find it nice to know the truth. Some connoisseurs opt for "Blow-Up": there is a sexy scene in which David Hemmings romps with a couple of naked teenagers. The Catholic Office gave "Blow-Up" a Condemned rating.

Most famous erotic movie star
This is Linda Lovelace, renowned for her performance in "Deep Throat", the most successful "pornographic" film to be shown in America. The film has been the subject of an obscenity charge in New York, a circumstance which may have helped it to gross some three and a half million dollars. The film focused on the discovery by a sex-conscious young woman that oral sex can be fun, and the plot hinges on her singular capacities in this direction.

First sex-film club in U.K.
The first sex-film club was the Compton in Old Compton Street; it opened in 1961 and was run by the former managers of a striptease club and a local cinema. The first films to be shown were based on nudist camps as locations – "The hero and heroine ended up holding hands and the sun set on yet another game of volleyball." The firm was eventually taken over by a large company and the name of the cinema was changed to Cinecenta.

First U.K. nudist film
There are those people who assert – and we know what they mean – that the nudist films have nothing to do with sex. Well, it may be so for some, but not for others. "The Garden of Eden", appropriately enough, was the first of the nudist pictures in Britain. It appeared in January 1957 and featured Jamie O'Hara. The film was sent around to the local authorities – "They didn't object, and there was considerable public acceptance of the picture, which opened the screens to nudity." **97**

Part IV

Aberrant Sex & Deviation

Most condemned as a perversion

Considering the number of "perversions" that are possible in human sexual behaviour it is amazing that *masturbation* should have been most condemned in history. One reason for this is undoubtedly that masturbation is common in any society whereas many other types of deviant sexuality are rare. It is hard to think of a disease or debilitating condition that has not been represented, at one time or another, as an effect of masturbation. The following are picked at random from quotes in Alex Comfort as supposed consequences of "self-abuse" – impotence, tabes dorsalis, pulmonary consumption, dyspepsia, dimness of sight, vertigo, epilepsy, hypochondriasis, loss of memory, fatuity, hysteria, asthma, melancholia, mania, dementia, paralysis and death! What is surprising is that *medical men* believed that such conditions could be caused by masturbation, a practice which – as we are told *ad nauseum* in these enlightened times – is entirely harmless.

Alex Comfort points out that masturbation concerned few medical writers prior to 1720 – and at least one writer saw it as a desirable practice. An anonymous author of "Hippolytus Redivivus" (1644) represented masturbation as a remedy against the dangerous allurements of Woman. Perhaps such an argument would not be popular today: at least it was preferable to the hysteria that was to follow in the eighteenth and nineteenth centuries!

Most famous male paedophile

Some older adults take sexual satisfaction in contact with children. Where such satisfaction is interpreted in general terms this is true of many parents, most of whom do not suspect that their affections are sexually based. In a more precise interpretation contact with children may be the only way in which some adults can experience orgasm. The following cases may fall into either of these categories. Lewis Carroll (C. L. Dodgson), the mathematical expert who created Alice, took immense pleasure (to what degree sexual?) in the company of little girls. His is perhaps the best-known example. Francis Kilvert, a clergyman who led a blameless life in the nineteenth century, wrote in his diary – "Shall I confess that I travelled ten

miles today over the hills for a kiss, to kiss that child's sweet face? Ten miles for a kiss!" After failure to consummate his marriage, John Ruskin became infatuated with a girl of ten.

Best attended orgies

Group sex, seemingly in fashion at the moment, has always had its adherents. In sex, as in most other things, there's nothing new under the sun. The largest number of group-sex participants almost certainly figured in religious orgies – where literally hundreds of half-crazed individuals could desport themselves in abandoned fashion. In the words of John Atkins in "Sex in Literature", "Mass copulation has always had its devotees, sometimes for the most admirable of reasons." The Bogomils and Fraticelli used to practise sexual promiscuity for the greater glory of God (though they probably enjoyed it themselves as well).

Most famous transvestite in history

The most famous example of transvestism in history was that of Chevalier d'Eon de Beaumont, a distinguished diplomat in the service of Louis XV. He was born in 1728 and died at the ripe old age of eighty-three, having spent forty-nine years as a man and thirty-four as a woman. Many people thought him to be an hermaphrodite. *Eonism* is sometimes taken as a synonym for *transvestism*.

"Fetishism" first introduced

According to Havelock Ellis, the term *erotic fetishism* was devised by Binet in 1888. Ellis had some interest in sexual terminology. He himself, for example, claimed to have invented the term "Eonism" for transvestism.

Most famous fetishist magazine in U.K.

"Rubber News" was sold in England not long ago. Gillian Freeman describes it on pp.165-166 of "The Undergrowth of Literature." Alas, by page 179 the magazine no longer exists. "Rubber News" was represented as "infinitely more comprehensive and interesting" than "even the best homosexual magazines." It even included its own Book Club – "Large publishers find that assured sales from a Book Club help to stabilize their costs and to give a reasonable guarantee of quantities. So why shouldn't a small publisher start a Book Club?" In June 1967 the Editor of "Rubber News" was fined £1000 for corrupting the innocent.

Most drastic case of urolognia

In 1949 John George Haigh admitted that he had murdered nine people, three of them complete strangers. In each case he opened a vein with a penknife, tapped off a glassful of blood, and drank it. He also liked the idea of drinking his own urine on account of the biblical text (John VII, 38) – "He that believeth in me, the Scripture hath said, out of his belly shall flow rivers of living water." It is well known that the drinking of urine can have a proudly erotic significance for some people. Havelock Ellis suffered (if that is the word) from urolagnia, as do a few writers to modern magazines such as "Forum".

Most drastic remedy for loss of maidenhood

In the nineteenth century, bands of young English gallants would seek out virgins. The demand generated a shameful trade in young girls. One problem was that there were just not enough available virgins to go around. An answer was to "manufacture" virgins, i.e. to sew up girls who had had previous sexual relations. Some poor young girls were treated in this fashion repeatedly, their maidenheads being restored after each coitus with a new client. In some areas of London disreputable surgeons specialized in "re-virginising" – and some girls were reported to have gone in for repairs as often as 500 times.

Most bizarre instance of white-slaving

There are many bizarre (and well-authen-ticated) tales from the world of *white-slaving*. One case was publicized at the trial of 1964 of three sisters of Mexico who, with immense brutality, ran a wholesale business of sex slavery. Girls were abducted – and then branded on the thigh or the breast with a red-hot iron; then they were locked up for months in tiny cells to break their spirits. When the girls were thought ready – through starvation, beating, and gross sexual exploitation – to satisfy any brothel frequenter they were sold to establishments in Mexico or elsewhere. Some girls were beaten to death; one was burned alive; some were buried or tied to a bed by means of barbed wire. At the ranch-house of the three sisters there was a makeshift crematorium in an oil-drum, in which the police discovered charred bones.

First wife-swapping magazine article

It was as late as 1957 that a magazine first decided to publish an article on wife-swapping. An issue of a men's magazine called "Mr.", published in New York and largely concerned with "seminude photos of bosomy females," carried a short article on this subject. In Brecher's words – wife-swapping is now a familiar term, "but it was fresh and attention-seeking back in 1957." The editor of "Mr." claimed it was this article that touched off the spate of similar articles in other magazines. "Mr." followed up the original article with a correspondence section, and many un-foreseen aspects of the phenomenon emerged, e.g. sex clubs devoted to trios, foursomes, or even larger groups. Soon magazines were carrying advertisements from people trying to contact other couples with a view to wife-swapping.

First recorded instance of sodomy in China

Sodomy is one of those ambiguous words. In American law, for instance, it can mean anything – from oral sex to anal inter-course. Generally *sodomy* is a synonym for *homosexuality*, implying the com-monplace homosexual act of anal intercourse. The first recorded instance of sodomy in Chinese history, figuratively described by the literati as "sharing the

peach" occurred in the State of Wei. Thus Duke Ling committed sodomy with a young court official, Mi Tzu-hsia, who had a face "as pretty as that of a blooming maiden."

Most famous biblical exhibitionist

The Bible, replete with sexual material gives us a number of superlatives. A famous exhibitionist case occurs with Noah who gets drunk and exposes himsel (Genesis IX, 21-25). Ham, Shem, and Japheth were horrified and tried to cover him up – "and their faces were backward, and they saw not their father's naked-ness." It must have been a close thing!

Most famous royal exhibitionist

Sexual display or exposure has not always been an oddity, a type of "perverted" or "deviant" sexuality. It used to be common and was even indulged in as a sign of respect to a visitor – as with the famous ladies of Ireland. The Queen of Ulster and all the ladies of the Court, to the number of 610, came to meet Cuchulainn, naked above the waist, and raising their skirts

HOMOSEXUALITY
First English-speaking lesbian organisation

The first open and avowed organization to cater exclusively for lesbian interests was in Britain. Established at the beginning of 1964 under the title, Minorities Research Group (M.R.G.), it followed an article, "A quick look at lesbians," by a journalist Dilys Rowe, which appeared in "Twentieth

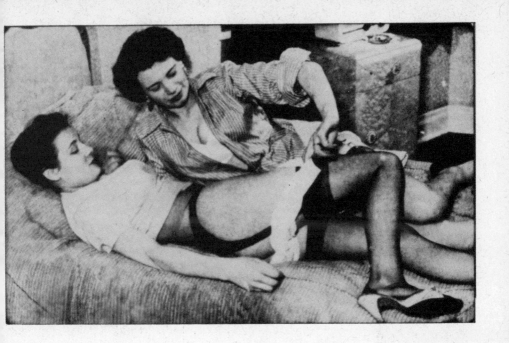

Century" (winter 1962-3, pp. 67-72). A lesbian was quoted as saying that "the thing that hurts a homosexual woman most is that the heterosexual does not recognize the spiritual quality of her love." Another lesbian replied in a subsequent issue of the magazine to the effect that what was resented was not that the spirituality of her life was doubted by the heterosexual, but its *authenticity*. The heterosexual does not realize how hard the homosexual woman finds it to imagine what it is to be in love with a man.

Most famous lesbian in history

The most famous lesbian in history is without doubt Sappho of Lesbos, born in the seventh century B.C. Praised by the Greeks for her sublime poetry she was variously depicted "the tenth Muse", "the marvel among women", etc. There is still debate as to whether she was truly an

exclusive homosexual or really bisexual, enjoying passionate relationships with both men and women. The life and poetry of Sappho – or Psappha, as she called herself in a local dialect – are filled with the love of women. She gathered a circle of girls around her; and with them she explored poetry, music and love. Inevitably the early Christians thought her highly immoral. Thus Saint Gregory of Nazianzus, Bishop of Constantinople, ordered her books to be burned wherever they were found, and he termed her "gynaeon pornikon erotomanes" ("lewd nymphomaniac"). In 1072 Pope Gregory destroyed more of her surviving works. The poems of Sappho that are still known today are said to represent about 5 per cent of her total output, the rest having been destroyed by the bigots.

Most famous 18th century lesbians

Two Irishwomen, Lady Eleanor Butler, whose brother was Earl of Ormonde, and Miss Sarah Ponsonby, a cousin of the Earl of Bessborough, pioneered a type of lesbian relationship in the eighteenth century. After becoming close friends at school they eloped but were brought back in disgrace and forbidden to communicate with each other in any way. Eventually, however, their relatives allowed them to live together and even made provision for a small allowance. They settled in a cottage in the Vale of Llangollen in North Wales – and, in consequence, became known as "The Ladies of Llangollen." Sometimes also called "The Platonists," they became the two most celebrated virgins in Europe and were visited by a host of famous people, including Sir Walter Scott and the Duke of Wellington.

Most famous speech in defence of homosexual love

Oscar Wilde, during his trial in 1895, declared – ' The love that dare not speak its name ' in this country, is such a great affection of an elder for a younger man as there was between David and Jonathan, such as Plato made the very basis of his philosophy, and such as you will find in the sonnets of Michelangelo and Shakespeare. It is that deep, spiritual affection that is as pure as it is perfect ... It is in this century misunderstood that it may be described as 'the love that dare not speak its name,' and on account of it I am placed where I am now. It is beautiful, it is fine, it is the noblest form of affection. There is nothing unnatural about it, and it repeatedly exists between an elder and a younger man, when the elder has intellect, and the younger man has all the joy, hope and glamour of life before him. That it should be so the world does not understand. The world mocks at it and sometimes puts one in the pillory for it.

"Queer" first used as "homosexual"

The word was first employed in 1925 in the American theatrical periodical called Variety. Other words soon followed, e.g. "gay," "camp" (from the Italian campeggiare, meaning to stand out from a background), "minny", "fairy", "queen", "fag", etc.

" GOD, I HATE BEING A FAIRY!"

First homosexual marriage

If marriage is desirable in any way that does not hinge upon procreation then there can be no reason in logic why the homosexual marriage should not exist as a social counterpart to the more frequent heterosexual equivalent. Some groups have urged such a course, and some societies have been prepared to tolerate such an arrangement. California has recently seen a homosexual marriage between two men, and not long ago – in 1969 – a priest in a Rotterdam church conducted a marriage service for two homosexuals.

Oscar Wilde by Aubrey Beardsley

"John, was it 1921 or 1922 that I was ravished by all those Tartars?"

RAPE
Raping chair first introduced

In Chinese eighteenth and nineteenth-century novels one often reads of a "romantic and comfortable chair". This device appears to have been much in use by outlaws and licentious landlords. It appears that the contraption was in the form of a collapsible chair, with automatic clasps fixed to its arms and legs. When a woman was put in the chair the clasps would spring to hold her arms and legs and then the chair would collapse to form a miniature bed. It appears that such chairs were much employed for raping purposes: the possession of them was made illegal under the Manchu rule. In 1949 peasants are said to have found such a chair in a landlord's mansion in Szechuan. The chair, possibly the last of its kind, was burned to ashes.

Most ancient Oriental technique

Tirad el-kebsh (the ram's attack) is the oldest known form of rape in the Orient. The Mongols were notorious for it, and there are numerous Chinese and Rajput prints showing Moghul warriors raping women and girls in this attitude. The female is thrown on her side, the assailant lifts her upper leg and squats between her thighs. Bernhard Stern, who observed this method among the Turks and Bosnian Muslims, notes that the rapist sometimes shifts position by lifting the girl's legs upon his shoulders like a yoke; whereupon he holds her thighs tight in his arms with all his might and, kneeling, "drives his sex organ into her, throwing himself upon her with all his weight, untroubled by her sighs and groans."

Most popular time

Various researchers have found that rape is more likely to occur in the warmer months of the year. Amir found that the number of forcible rapes in the U.S. tended to increase during the hot summer months. Summer was also noted as the time when multiple rapes are most likely to occur. Uniform Crime Reports also show a higher incidence of rape in the warmer spring and summer months. A study of rape in Denmark – by Svalastoga, covering 1946-56 – reached similar conclusions.

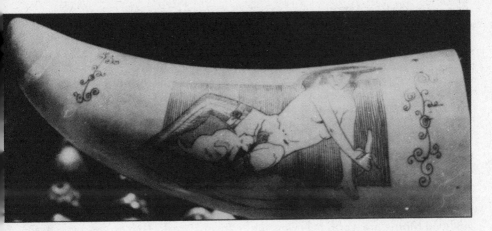

Least popular time

You are least likely to be raped around the December/January period, according to the various studies cited in H. M. McDonald's "Rape Offenders And Their Victims". This doesn't mean you won't be raped as part of the Christmas festivities, just that it is less likely than on an equally festive occasion in the middle of the summer. Efforts have been made to draw conclusions about a correlation between revealed sexual behaviour (rape being one type) and the biological tide at any season of the year. Such ideas are not all that successful.

BESTIALITY

Most famous medieval tale

A famous tale is told by Peter Damain in his "De bono religiosi status et variorum animatium tropologia". The eleventh century story concerns a Count Gulielmus who had both a pet ape and a wanton wife. In due course the ape became her lover. One day the ape became so mad with jealousy on seeing the count lying with his wife that it attacked him, wounding him so badly that he died. Damain had been told about this incident by Pope Alexander II who had also shown him a monster which was supposed to be the offspring of the countess sired by the ape. The monster, an ape-like boy, had been called Maimo after his simian father.

First instanced as public entertainment

Bestiality was a common form of entertainment in the Roman arena – in the words of

A scrimshaw, an ivory task traditionally carved and inked by a sailor. It is about four inches in length.

R. E. L. Masters in "The Prostitutes In Society", mass bestiality, as public display in Rome, was "a phenomenon unique in all of history". Beasts were specially trained to copulate with women: if the girls or women were unwilling then the animal would attempt rape. A surprising range of creatures was used for such purposes – bulls, giraffes, leopards,

"For heaven's sake, Augustus, they haven't even started yet."

107

cheetahs, wild boar, zebras, stallions, jack-asses, huge dogs, apes, etc. The beasts were taught how to copulate with a human being either via the vagina or via the anus. In the modern world occasional shows are staged where an animal copulates with a woman but there has never been anything comparable to what was seen in the Roman arena.

Most prevalent tales of human seduction by animals

A variety of animals have supposedly made sexual advances to human beings. A few of the accounts – e.g. those of Kohler and Desmond Morris, are worth believing. But some are clearly fictitious. The baboon has often been represented as a seducer of women. Perhaps the most famous tale in this context is that entitled The King's Daughter and the Ape, from the Arabian classic "The Thousand Nights and a Night." In his translation, Sir Richard Burton mentions that in his opinion the ape referred to is probably the cynocephalus (Baboon), a beast "with a natural penchant for women".

Most frequent incidence

Kinsey found that the most frequent incidence of animal coitus, i.e. human/animal sexual intercourse, was in excess of eight times a week – and this for the age-group of under fifteen years!

Least likely animals

Men and women have tried to have sexual relations with a wide variety of non-human animals. Some of the creatures are common domestic pets. Some are less common – and it says something for human imagination and ingenuity that sex was ever thought of in connection with them! Roman women used the heads of live snakes. Herzog tell us of women who used the tails of live fishes for insertion in the vagina. Some women have smeared honey on the vulva to attract flies. Thus in Stekel we find – "The flies thus attracted by the honey would tickle her until her sexual appetite was appeased." Men also have used flies for sexual titillation.

In mythology, Leda was "visited" by Zeus in the form of a swan.

Best documented case among Trobrianders

The Trobrianders of North-West Melanesia gained lasting fame through the anthropological researches of Bronislaw Malinowski ("The Sexual Life of Savages"). It is quite possible that we know more about the sexual propensities and beliefs of a number of primitive communities than we do about our own complex but confused society. The Trobrianders yielded up their secrets to Malinowski. At least one well-documented case of bestiality is on record. In this instance a man copulated with a dog: the names of both man and dog were house-hold words in the villages. The culprit, Moniyala, apparently lived down his shame. "The subject of his past lapse, however, must never be mentioned in his presence, for, the natives say, if he heard anyone speaking about it he would commit *lo'u* (suicide by jumping from a tree)."

Most famous Oriental type

Chinese lovers – in pre-Mao days – were said to be fond of fowl. Mantegazza has remarked that "The Chinese are famous for their love affairs with geese ..." This would be remarkable enough: the actual *way* the Orientals used such a creature for sexual purposes is even more extraordinary. At the moment of ejaculation the man would pull the head off the live animal to get "the pleasurable benefit of the anal sphincter's last spasms in the victim." De Sade has commented that a turkey was used in the same way in Parisian brothels, where the act was termed *avisodomy*. As well as causing desirable anal spasms in the poor bird, its body temperature was thought to rise as a consequence of losing a head, thus giving further titillation. Of a number of famous practitioners of this form of bestiality, one was Tipoo Sahib, the Sultan and "Tiger" of Mysore, the scourge of the British.

1

2

3

4

Society most tolerant to bestiality

We are all supposed to condemn bestiality, though only rarely are sound medical or psychological factors advanced (See "British Jnl. Sexual Medicine", Jan./Feb. 1974, p. 43). Some societies, however, have not been quick to condemn sexual intercourse with animals. Ford and Beach mention the Copper Eskimoes who used to live on the Arctic Coast of North America. These people apparently had no aversion to intercourse with live or dead animals. Bestiality was also common among the Hopi Indians, the Masai, etc. Among the Fez there was a magic so powerful that it allowed a man to "deflower seventy-two virgin cows" in one night. K. Rasmussen has recorded a tale of the Eskimoes: "There was once a woman who would not have a husband. Her family let dogs copulate with her. They took her out to an island, where the dogs then made her pregnant. After that she gave birth to white men. Before that there had been no white men." The fishermen of the East African coast from the Red Sea to the Indian Ocean have regular coitus with the carcasses of the female dugong, an herbivorous aquatic mammal about eight feet in length. The vagina of the female is said to resemble anatomically that of a woman. Coitus with the carcass is thought to be necessary to "lay the ghost" of the creature: otherwise it might pursue the hunter. It was for this sort of reason that the ancient Egyptians and various other peoples committed sodomy on the bodies of fallen enemies.

MASTURBATION

Most dangerous techniques

Men and women will go to great lengths to give themselves sexual satisfaction. Sometimes the results are not what was hoped for. One book mentions the case of a man who tried to masturbate by putting his penis into the sucking end of a vacuum-cleaner. The result was that all the skin was sucked off the penis. This method of masturbation "is not therefore recommended." P. Mantegazza has instanced the case of a penis caught in a bayonet tube and in the bath tub faucet. Many similar such cases are known to doctors and diligent researchers.

Highest frequency

According to Kinsey maximum masturbation rates were to be found in children under the age of fifteen. For this age group the maximum frequency of masturbation was in excess of twenty-three times a week. Some females surveyed had experienced orgasm from this source as many as thirty or more times in a week. Some energetic females had masturbated to orgasm as many as one hundred times in a single hour! But some women only tried it once a month. Kinsey concluded that "the range of variation in almost every type of sexual activity seems to be far greater among females."

Youngest participant

There is copious evidence (much of it quoted by Kinsey) of children masturbating at all ages from a few months old onwards. Kinsey mentions one record of a seven-month-old infant and records of five infants under one year of age who were observed in masturbation. Some of the cited evidence includes Townsend (five cases under one year of age); Talmey (one case of nine months); Spitz (rocking and genital play observed in over half of 248 children under one year of age), etc.

Most popular fantasy

Among masturbating females sixty per cent, according to Kinsey, indulge in heterosexual fantasy. This is hardly surprising since most females are heterosexual; only ten per cent of women had homosexual fantasies while masturbating.

Least popular fantasy

Not many women fantasize about sexual contact with animals. In the Kinsey survey only one per cent of women masturbated while fantasizing about animals. Four times as many as this had sadomasochistic fantasies during "self-stimulation."

Most frequent by social class

One of the curious things about sexual behaviour is that it correlates – in frequency, variety, etc. – with social class. Kinsey found that masturbation was more common in educated classes than in those

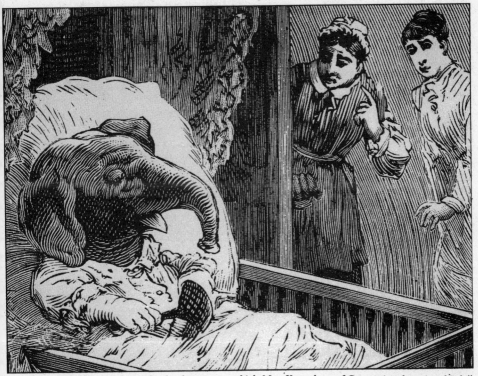

"The extraordinary freak of nature to which Mrs. Kretschner of Connecticut has given birth."

groups concerned with unskilled or manual labour. Of all classes the professional groups masturbate most.

ADULTERY
Oddest means of detection

Men have always been keen to detect adultery in their wives – or, by means of chastity belts, etc., to prevent them the opportunity. Some odd ways of dicovering the unfaithful wife have been invented. Some have relied on magic, e.g. the test which makes use of the supposed power of holy water. There is a nice description of such an "adultery test" in Numbers V. We will quote one bit – "And when he hath made her to drink the water, then it shall come to pass, that if she be defiled, and have done trespass against her husband, that the water that causeth the curse shall enter into her, and become bitter, and her belly shall swell, and her thigh shall rot: and the woman shall be a curse among her people." As one couple of writers remark – "God did not trouble to institute any similar test for unfaithful husbands."

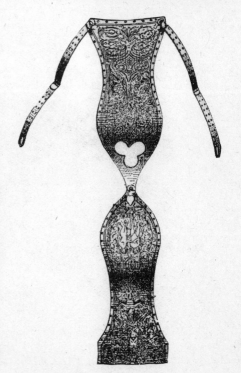

111

Most snobbish excuse

Adultery has not always been condemned in history. There are a number of mitigating circumstances. Sometimes it is even desirable, from an ethical point-of-view, that a couple commit adultery. Great love has often been taken as sanctifying sex outside marriage! Another excuse is that one is offering onself to a high-born person. This argument would be hard to advance in the modern world, but there was a time when it had a certain vogue. In medieval times folk sometimes saw things in an odd way – "Gawain praises the good taste of his own lady-love, Orgueilleuse, for having offered her favours to so valiant a warrior as the Red Knight." In a Provençal romance, a husband reproaches his wife for her infidelity. She replies: "My Lord, you have no dishonour on that account, for the man I love is a noble baron, expert in arms, namely Roland, the nephew of King Charles." The husband is reduced to silence by the explanation and is filled with confusion at his unseemly interference.

"Les Baisers" by Joseph-Maria Lambeaux

CUNNILINGUS & FELLATIO
Only Royal example

There is no reason to suppose that royal personages do not enjoy their sex the same as the rest of us. Apart from the occasional scandal, however, we know very little of the sexual predilictions of reigning monarchs: sometimes, after the event, some information leaks out. There is one nice case on record – of royal oral sex. The T'ang Dynasty Empress Wu Hu, evidently a keen feminist, designed a sexual custom aimed at elevating the female and humbling the male. To her, *fellatio* represented suposed masculine supremacy: so she devised a means whereby "licking of the lotus stamen" could be exalted into prime extracoital importance and thus symbolize the advent of feminine domination. Wu Hu insisted that all governmental officials and visiting dignitaries pay homage to her Imperial Highness by performing cunnilingus upon her. Thus old paintings depict the empress holding her robe open while a dignitary kneels before her to lick her genitals (A. Edwardes & R. E. L. Masters, "The Cradle of Erotica").

... AND ANOTHER THING —
THIS HABIT OF TALKING
OUT OF THE SIDE OF
YOUR MOUTH.

Most famous fellatrice in Ancient Egypt

A fellatrice is a woman – often a prostitute – who specializes in the art of *fellatio,* i.e. exciting the male genitals by means of mouth, lips, and tongue. Cleopatra of Egypt has been represented as the "most famous free-love fellatrice of the ancient world." Cleo is said (I do not know how reliable the authority) to have perfomed fellatio on a thousand men. Perhaps this is why the Greeks chose to call her *Meri-chane* (Gaper) – "she who gapes wide for ten thousand men; the wide-mouthed one; the ten-thousand mouthed woman." Cleopatra was also known as *Cheilon* (Thick-Lipped). It was said that she fellated a hundred Roman noblemen in one night. (A. Edwardes & R. E. L. Masters).

Highest quoted number of positions

There are literally an infinite number of positions for any form of sexual activity. This means that there is no upper limit to the number of ways that, e.g. oral sex, can be performed. This rather liberal way of interpreting sexual postures leads to odd consequences. Legman, for instance, has suggested that there are 14,288,400 positions for cunnilingus alone! This strikes me as rather perplexing. Is he sure that there are not 14,288,401?

Most famous fricatrices

We have already met the fellatrice: the fricatrice, her younger sister, concentrates on *rubbing* the male genitals – which can be nice. The Jewesses of North Africa are supposed to have enjoyed a reputation for this sort of thing. Such females were also found among the inhabitants of Lesbos and were described by Catullus as standing at crossways and in alleys "to jerk off the high-souled sons of Rome." In eighteenth-century France the skilled fricatrice was well-known. In the United States, by contrast, "the fricatrice has never enjoyed any vogue. Practical Americans, if they want to masturbate, do it themselves. . . ."

INCEST
Highest incidence

Incest, evoking a variety of taboo responses, is condemned equally in primitive and advanced societies. International incidences have been reported as high as five per million population per year, and isolated pockets within a nation have been even higher, i.e. seven per million in the State of Washington. New Zealand has the record with a figure of nine per million population per year.

Lowest incidence

The lowest international incidence of incest is one per million per year. In the United States, Weinberg has reported incidences ranging from 1.2 cases per million in 1910 to 1.1 per million in 1930. It has been shown that incest frequency diminishes during war and increases during postwar periods. The crime is infrequent in all types of societies – some communities (e.g. the Mormons) and some primitive races have permitted incestuous unions. It has also prevailed historically in the social elites of many countries.

113

Most famous biblical instance

In *Genesis* XX, 12, we learn that Abraham married his father's daughter –"And yet indeed she is my sister; she is the daughter of my father, but not the daughter of my mother, and she became my wife."

Most famous unpunished case

In ancient Rome the laws against incest, like many Roman laws, were harsh. In the early years of the Republic, people who had committed incest were forced to kill themselves. And in the first century B.C., offenders were thrown from the cliffs at Tarpei. Constantine's sons also imposed the death penalty, and Theodosius (A.D. 379-395), who made Christianity the state religion, used death by burning. Perhaps the most famous *unpunished* case of incest in ancient Rome is that of Caligula (A.D. 37–47), who married his sister Agrippina, who, as the wife of Claudius and Dowager Empress also had sexual relations with her own son by an earlier marriage, the future Emperor Nero.

Most tolerant societies

Summer cited in "Folkways" a whole series of primitive cultures and groups from various societies in which incest is allowed or tolerated, and ones in which there is not even a concept of incest. As one example, certain hill-tribes in Cambodia allow brothers and sisters to marry; as another, the Indian Kukis look favourably on all incestuous relations except those between mother and son.

SADISM/MASOCHISM
Most famous masochist

Leopold von Sacher-Masoch, born in 1836, was not the *first* masochist, despite the title of the book by J. Cleugh ("The First Masochist"). Centuries before the arrival of Sacher-Masoch men and women would surely have discovered that in certain cases apparent suffering had the power to generate sexual delight. Count Leopold did however give his name to the phenomenon, and it is on this circumstance that his fame largely rests. This is, perhaps, a pity. He was after all a successful novelist – with over ninety titles to his credit. He was also said to be fond of children and cats.

Word first coined

Just as Sacher-Masoch gave his name to masochism so the Marquis de Sade gave his name to sadism. There is controversy as to the extent to which de Sade was a practising sadist. Did he in reality act out his fantasies or were his novels the main vehicles for his sexual imaginings? De Sade like Sacher-Masoch, wrote books of merit; yet he is not remembered for these. The world inevitably associates him with sexual "perversion," but such a thing only touches part of the man – in addition to whatever sexual propensities he had he also possessed considerable political and philosophical stature. His life is a depressing catalogue of frustration, thwarted ambition, and imprisonment.

Most famous female sadist

Our woman sadist, unlike de Sade, was a practising person, i.e. she wrote no books but killed and tortured to her heart's content. In 1611, aged fifty, the Hungarian noblewoman Erzsebet Bathory was walled up alive in her castle in the Minor Carpathians for having killed some six hundred young girls in various ways. The judge at her trial appears to have been particularly concerned that she murdered noblewomen as well as mere servant-girls. Bathory used a number of ingenious devices. For instance, she put a terrified naked girl in a narrow iron cage equipped with inward-pointing spikes to pierce the victim: then Bathory would hoist the cage to the ceiling and sit beneath to enjoy the rain of blood that came down. Another device was a robot – wearing real teeth torn from a servant – designed to clasp a victim in a tight embrace, whereupon sharp spikes would shoot out from the robot: the blood of the victim ran down a channel, was warmed over a fire, and collected for the countess's bath.

Most bizarre invention

There have been many sadistic inventions: the medieval torture chambers were full of them. We need not give a list here. Suffice it to mention that the inquisitors, with full theological sanction, thought it proper to introduce a clamp specially devised for the torture of pregnant women. In more recent times, electrical generators have

Fanciful representation of the Marquis de Sade, for it has not been established that the man did practise sadism.

been used on all parts of the bodies of men and women. And Chapman Pincher mentions (in "Sex in Our Time") a pair of binoculars in the Black Museum of Scotland Yard – "These were sent anonymously through the post to a girl, and by chance her father turned the adjusting screw before she put them to her eyes. A pair of spring-loaded penknife blades shot out of the eyepieces."

115

PROSTITUTION
Most famous English call-girl
This is almost certainly Christine Keeler, born in 1942, the British call-girl at the centre of the "Profumo Affair" scandal of 1963. She left home at 16, met Stephen Ward, and later became involved in a wide range of sexual activities in the Ward circle – nude parties, group sex, flagellation, voyeurism, etc. Christine met John Profumo, then Secretary of State for War, at Cliveden: he was attracted to her after seeing her swimming nude in the pool of Lord Astor. After a security warning Profumo stopped seeing Christine, but later lied about the affair to the House of Commons. Ward, deserted by Christine and arrested for living off immoral earnings, committed suicide before he was convicted. Christine sold her story to the "News of the World" for £23,000.

Most popular English prostitute
Nell Gwynne has been represented as "the only darling strumpet of the warm-hearted British public". Swinburne wrote of her –
> "Nell Gwynne
> Sweet heart, that no taint of the throne
> or the stage
> Could touch with unclean transforma-
> tion, or alter

> To the likeness of courtiers whose con-
> sciences falter
> At the smile or the frown, at the mirth
> or the rage,
> Of a master whom chance could
> inflame or assuage,
> Our Lady of Laughter, invoked in no
> psalter,
> Praise be with thee yet from a hag-
> ridden age.
> Our Lady of Pity thou wast: and to thee
> All England, whose sons are the sons of
> the sea,
> Give thanks, and will not hear if history
> snarls.
> When the name of the friend of her
> sailors is spoken;
> And thy lover she cannot but love – by
> the token
> That thy name was the last on the lips of
> King Charles."

She was born in 1650. In 1665 she appeared on the stage as Cydaria in Dryden's "Indian Emperor".

Most successful 18th century whore
Kitty – "one of the most beautiful and talented *demi-mondaines* of the eighteenth century" – moved in such wealthy circles that she could command the

Left to right: Christine Keeler; Nell Gwynn; a London brothel in 18th century.

extraordinary sum of 100 guineas a night. The Duke of York, after spending a night with Kitty, gave her a mere fifty-pound note, since it was all he had with him. She promptly dismissed him and refused to receive him again. To further show her contempt, she sent the banknote to a pastry chef with instructions that it be baked into a tart and served up for breakfast.

Most successful 19th century whore

Laura Bell, ex-Belfast shop girl, whose apogee as what Sir William Hardman called "The Queen of London Whoredom" occurred in the mid-nineteenth century, was an immensely successful prostitute. When she visited the Opera in 1852 the whole house rose to watch her departure. In 1856 she married Captain Augustus Thistlethwaytes, a nephew of the then Bishop of Norwich. They lived for a time in Grosvenor Square in what may be considered a somewhat eccentric fashion. The Captain, for instance, summoned servants by firing a pistol through the bedroom ceiling. Laura had brought to the marriage a dowry of £250,000, earned from a Nepalese prince. Later she "got religion" and "she was, by all accounts, as successful a preacher as she had been a whore – no

mean achievement." Cora Pearl, another nineteenth-century prostitute managed to accumulate a few hundred thousand pounds.

Most famous biblical client

The powerful and wealthy Judah praised and worshipped by his brethren (*Genesis* XLIX, 8), slept with a harlot (*Genesis* XXXVIII, 18), and made no secret of the fact. The Bible is truly a compound of immense sexual license and sternest sexual prohibition – possibly the one generated the other.

Highest status accorded to prostitutes

Many societies, ancient and modern, have made provision for high-ranking prostitutes (we have already met Kitty and Laura Bell). The Greek *hetairai* were a class of high-status prostitutes as were the English and French courtesans. The temple-harlots of ancient Babylon (mentioned in Herodotus) had their own high status in society, as did the Japanese geishas. In ancient China high-class prostitutes were classified as *ch'ing-kuan-jen* and *hung-kuang-jen* (pure official attendants and popular official attendants respectively), since in the Manchu Dynasty their impor- 117

Ancient Chinese brothel

prostitutes was uncovered by the police. Amputees have also been immensely popular. Not so long ago a woman with one leg was operating in the San Francisco area: "she claimed to have more business than she could handle." Hunchbacks and women with one or both breasts amputated have also been immensely popular. Similarly some men apparently desire a woman with a club foot or females with hideous scars. And hermaphrodite or trans-sexual prostitutes have also been much in demand.

Youngest prostitute

Child prostitution has always existed in history. Temple harlots were as young as six and seven; and in China boys as young as four years were trained "in the fine art of passive pederasty;" girl and boy brothels were common in the ancient world and in more modern times also. The Chinese boy prostitutes were sanctified by *Tcheou-Wang*, God of Sodomy. Without doubt the youngest prostitutes of all were the babies in the brothels of ancient Rome. It has been noted that "sucking babes" were introduced into the brothels. The Emperor Domitian was praised when he attempted to stamp out all forms of infant prostitution. In the Japanese *Yoshiwara* or Whores' Quarter, little girls were kept for fellatio. The high-status geishas, contrary to some imaginings, were only available for vaginal coitus.

Most immoral use of army funds

Soldiers and sailors have always been keen to frequent prostitutes. This is as true of the modern conscripts in foreign lands as it is of the enlisted man in the armies of antiquity. One startling use of campaign funds was brought to the attention of Richard I at the beginning of a European enterprise. "When Richard arrived at Marseilles he found that the English knights who had preceded him had squandered all the campaign funds on prostitutes."

Most prevalent in London

Those pessimistic souls who declare with paradoxical relish that the nation's morals have never been worse should take time off to glance at the extent of Victorian

tant customers were mainly high officials. It is a sobering thought that the derogatory connotation of the word *prostitute* springs mainly from the influence of the Judeo-Christian tradition. Many societies in history have viewed things differently.

Most bizarre animal prostitutes

In a number of the ancient temples a variety of animals were trained to copulate with women and to have intercourse *per anum* with men. Monkeys and baboons were encouraged to play with the genitals of both sexes. Attending priests accepted the customer's payment for this service. Use was also made of such creatures as dogs and goats in various establishments. In more recent times geese and turkeys have been placed at the disposal of frequenters of brothels in various parts of the world. A more frequent use of animals is in erotic displays: dogs, small horses, etc. have been made to copulate with women in front of a paying audience. Such practices still take place today.

Most bizarre human prostitutes

Every imaginable type of human being has been required for purposes of prostitution. In Italy a ring of grand-mother-

Male brothel, circa 1907

Child prostitutes, a feature of history, and sanctified in China.

English prostitution. Archenholtz talked of the 50,000 prostitutes in London, Marylebone alone having no less than 13,000 (such figures are generally thought to be exaggerated). The Kronhausens reckoned that the number of prostitutes in the London of Walter's days was around 80,000 (in a total London population of only about two million). If we add to this figure the estimated number of "semi" – or *occasional* prostitutes we find a figure of something like 100,000 – 150,000 women engaged in full-time or part-time prostitution at the height of the Victorian era in the London district alone!

first recorded instances of such types of prostitution are for the Mesopotamia of 2300 B.C. From this region it spread throughout the Near East.

Most exclusive "Love Club"

The English Aphrodites comprised an eighteenth-century Love Club – which arranged wife-swapping and a variety of other sexual diversions. Membership was £10,000 for a gentleman and £5,000 for a lady, plus a gift compatible with economic status. Fortunately the journal of a female member has been preserved. She provides a list of 4,959 amorous rendezvous for a period of twenty years. Among her lovers were –

```
 72 princes and prelates
 93 rabbis
439 monks
288 commoners
  2 uncles
119 musicians
929 officers
342 financiers
420 society men
117 valets
 12 cousins
 47 negroes
and 1,614 foreigners.
```

Oldest form

The oldest type of prostitution must have been the ancient form of "street-walking," where a woman clearly desported herself in the hope of financial or other reward. It is likely that there are professions as old as prostitution, but unlikely that there are any older. It has even been suggested that a form of prostitution can be detected in pre-human animal communities: for example, if a baboon offers herself sexually to a male she may at the same time contrive to steal his food – he may detect this but tolerate the transaction!

Earliest in a temple

Sacred temple prostitution existed throughout the bulk of the ancient world. It has been described for Egypt, Babylon, Greece, etc. and was generally seen as **120** having deep religious significance. The

First publicly administered

Solon, the law-giver, introduced the first publicly administered brothel in the Athens of 550 B.C. The brothel, soon copied in nearby cities, was run by slaves; and the inmates were also slaves, the lowest class of Greek prostitute. From the taxes collected from the licensed brothels (Dicteria), Solon built a temple to the Goddess Aphrodite. There is a passage in Athenaeus to show the gratitude of the citizens for Solon's wisdom in establishing a brothel which would give an outlet to lustful impulse without endangering the social order –

Solon, you were a true benefactor of humanity, for our city is full of young men with exuberant passions that might spur them on to criminal excesses. However, you bought women, provided them with everything they might need, and put them in places where they

Up in the world

Down on her luck

would be available to all who wanted them. They are as nature made them; no surprises, everything on view! Isn't that something? To open the door, all you need is an obolus. Have a go – no false modesty or coyness, no fear that they'll run away. You can have it now if you want it, and whatever way you like it . . .

These fillies to Cypris, built for sport, stand in a row one behind the other, their dresses sufficiently undone to let all the charms of nature be seen, like the nymphs nurtured by the Eridanus in its pure waters. For a few pence, you can purchase a moment of bliss with no risks attached . . .

There are thin ones, thick ones, round ones, tall ones, curved ones; young, old, middle-aged, mature as you wish – yours for the taking, and you don't need to bring along a ladder or sneak in through a hole in the roof . . . If you are old they'll call you "Daddy" if you are young it will be "little brother." At any rate there they are where anyone can have them without fear, day or night . . .

First institutionalized in China
Prostitution in China is certainly as old as human life in that part of the world. But as a thorough-going institutionalized form it can first be dated to the Feudal Period of 841–221 B.C. At that time the aristocracy keep huge numbers of courtesans, paid companions, actors and musicians, not merely for use but as status symbols. The courtesans were chosen for abilities which could be sexual, musical, poetic, etc.

First established in the English Court
Court brothels existed during the time of Charlemagne and later a well-equipped brothel was established by contemporaries of George III. This latter establishment comprised a group of houses near St. James's Palace, in a lane called "King's Place": the employed girls were only allowed to walk. in the royal parks, and only the *innermost circle of the court* was allowed to frequent the court brothel.

Least expected benefactors
It may seem odd that royal courts should have established their own brothels, but most of us know that such was done. Similarly, in our prudish times the idea of *municipal* brothels may appear somewhat startling; but again we know that such an arrangement was commonplace in times 121

past. What is also interesting is that the Armed Forces made special provision for prostitution. Thus, in the Army and Navy Estimates of 1870–1871, no less than $110,000 was set aside for 2700 registered prostitutes in eighteen naval and military stations. And the London Stock Exchange maintained its own brothel in the eighteenth century.

Brothels first introduced in England

Again it all depends what you mean by . . . Henry II organized the "stews" (bathhouses with opportunity for sex) in 1161. And the famous "seraglios" were introduced in 1750. A certain Mrs. Goadby had visited the French *sérails*, esp. those of Justine, Paris and Montigny: in all such establishments high standards were maintained; many beautiful girls were employed with various talents. Mrs. Goadby even went so far as to employ a physician to look after the health of the girls; and she imported fine silks from France. The result of such enterprise was that she became extremely wealthy and later retired to the country.

Most famous homosexual brothel in 19th century England

This brothel was opened by a certain Charles Hammond around 1884 in a house off the Tottenham Court Road. It was soon doing well and included a number of aristocratic and well-to-do homosexuals. It was suspected that one of the clients was the 25-year-old Prince Eddy, later Duke of Clarence, eldest son of the Prince of Wales. One speciality in this establishment was the "telegraph boy", willing both to sleep with customers and to deliver telegrams; they earned a few shillings a week by all their efforts! Eventually the police raided the place. Hammond escaped but Veck (a 40-year-old clergyman) and Newlove (an 18-year-old clerk) were given four months and nine months in jail respectively.

NECROPHILIA
Word first coined
Necrophilia was a word coined in 1860 by Dr. Guislain to define a category of

"insane destroyers." In 1901 Epaulard suggested that anyone who loved corpses, platonically or not, should be called a "necrophile." The word *necrophagy* was invented in 1875 by W. A. F. Browne who reckoned it an instance of cannibalism without any erotic connotations. Epaulard was sure however that it had erotic significance. The necrophage is taken as different from the cannibal inasmuch as the latter chooses the man he is going to eat while the victim is still alive. *Necrosadism* was a term invented by Epaulard in 1901 to designate those who mutilated corpses. The sadism in a case of this sort is only apparent as the victim can experience no pain. The corpse fulfills the purpose of a fetish. (O. Volta, "The Vampire").

Most famous cases

There are many historical instances of men and women in love with corpses. Thus the tyrant Periandrus lived a year with the dead Melissa. Herod was said to have slept for seven years next to his dead wife Mariamne. And as Charlemagne grew older he would not be parted from the remains of his German mistress. Queen Juana of Castile kept the corpse of her husband Philip the Handsome near her from 1506 to 1509. The ancient Egyptians, knowing full well the sexual attractiveness of a dead body to some folk, never let the embalmers near a corpse until several days after the death.

Most famous case of sexual cannibalism

This form of cannibalism has featured in a number of court cases. Ornella Volta gives us a number of graphic cases in which cannibalism has been linked to sexual pleasure. Gilles Garnier killed a young girl with his hands and teeth, and took a piece of her flesh home to his wife. A certain Andrea Bichel murdered little girls and was recorded as saying, "as I tore open their chests I was so excited that I wanted to tear off a piece of flesh and eat it." Tirsch boiled human flesh before eating it and Antoine Leger ate it raw. The following court dialogue has been quoted by Volta –

Judge: But what did you want to do with this little girl?

"How about us going bump in the night?"

Leger: Eat her up, your Honour.

Judge: And why did you drink her blood?

Leger: I was thirsty, your honour.

Only instances of necrophilia in Greek antiquity

Licht "can only quote three passages from Grecian antiquity;" Dimœtes had sexual intercourse with a drowned girl; Herodotus relates how an Egyptian embalmer "misused the dead body of a beautiful woman;" and he also tells us how Periander committed an offense on the dead body of his wife Melissa after he had – perhaps accidentally – killed her.

FLAGELLATION
First organized processions

By the eleventh century the Franciscans were extolling self-flagellation as a penance. And the Italian Benedictine St. Pietro Damian organized group flagellation for laymen. Two hundred years later a procession of fanatical flagellants – closely linked to the Flagellant sect – set out under the auspices of St. Anthony of Padua. This austere saint, theologian and preacher – keen to combat manifest sexuality – was in fact adding to the sexual ferment. In 1260 unofficial processions of voluntary scourgers, each member heartily whipping the man in front of him, started streaming through Italy and out into northern and central Europe. The participants, all male, carried banners and candles, and they sang as they marched.

First ecclesiastical exhortation

Towards the end of the eleventh century the church was exhorting ordinary men and women to chastise themselves as a form of penance. Whipping or scourging was becoming increasingly popular, and the clerics were keen that such practices should not remain the prerogative of the inmates of nunneries and monasteries. As we have seen, it was St. Pietro Damian who first organised group flagellation for laymen. In the superstitious and fearful atmosphere of the times we may suppose that many volunteers came forward, a substantial number of whom would have derived sexual satisfaction from a mode of chastisement meant to cure them of carnal thoughts.

Most curious 17th century account

In 1671 a small publication appeared entitled "Whipping Tom Brought to light, **123**

Lesbian flagellation. England is reputed to be the natural home of the art of flagellation.

and exposed to capital Views: In an account of several late Adventures of the pretended Whipping Spirit". It seems that the streets of London had been haunted by a phantom spanker, who had been nicknamed "Whipping Tom." He would lurk in dark corners and, grabbing a passing wench, he would toss up her petticoats and spank her vigorously until she cried for help. Then he would run off like a thief into the night. Until finally captured he was assumed to have supernatural powers.

Most sadistic 19th century book

One of the most sadistic books of the nineteenth century was entitled, "Experimental Lecture, By Colonel Spanker, on the Exciting and Voluptuous Pleasures to be derived from crushing and humiliating the spirit of a beautiful and modest young lady; as delivered by him in the assembly room of the Society of Aristocratic Flagellants." The book recounts the experiences of Colonel Spanker and his cronies. According to Spanker's philosophy there can be no true enjoyment in whipping lower-class women, prostitutes, or any other victims who willingly submit themselves. Accordingly, Spanker and his band capture a beautiful seventeen-year-old blonde and lock her up in a house in Mayfair. There she is subjected to all forms of brutal torture and sexual maltreatment. A contemporary critic called the book "the most coldly cruel and unblushingly indecent of any we have ever read ... in the English language."

Most typical 19th century book

The eighteenth and nineteenth centuries saw the production of a wide range of flagellant material in England. A book held by one writer to be "the most typical" of all the late nineteenth century English flagellant novels was a book called "The Mysteries of Verbena House: or, Miss Bellasis birched for thieving." The author signed himself simply Etonensis. A critic

1905 advertisement in "Le Rire" for bibliophiles of all tastes in the area of aberrant and deviant sex.

remarked – "After wading through so many dull, insipid, if not absolutely repulsive books on the subject, it is a relief to alight at last upon one which tact and clever writing render almost readable."

Most famous female flagellant
There were many high-class brothels in the nineteenth century. One of the most famous of these was run by a Mrs. Theresa Berkley (or Berkeley) of 28 Charlotte Street. She was a "governess", i.e. she specialized in chastisement, whipping, flagellation, and the like. She was even credited with the invention of the *Berkley horse*, an ingenious flogging machine that earned her a fortune. One writer (B. J. Hurwood in "The Golden Age of Erotica") said of her – "She possessed the first requisite of a courtezan, viz., lewdness; for without a woman is positively lecherous she cannot keep up the affectation of it, and it will soon be perceived that she moves her hands or her buttocks to the tune of pounds, shillings, and pence".

Country where most prevalent
England has long been represented as the natural home of flagellation. Thus, "Perhaps it was the cold climate which originally aroused in Englishmen a desire for whipping." "Nowhere in the world do we find such a deep affection for the rod." (B. J. Hurwood "The Golden Age of Erotica") And again – "Flagellation-mania (the desire to beat and flog) and preference for the use of the rod may be described as a specifically English abuse; it was so widespread among all ranks and ages that it formed one of the most interesting features of their sexual life." (I. Bloch "Sexual Life in England") Many writers have suggested that flagellation is common in England as nowhere else. There is yet, I feel, a need for a cross-cultural study in rigorous empirical terms. **125**

Part V

Animals & Plants

First plants to reproduce bisexually

It is surprising how many people are not aware, even today, that plants reproduce bisexually in many species. In fact the plants have been at it a long time. Algae first began to reproduce bisexually around 1,000,000,000 years ago. Considering that man has been copulating for a million years or so, the various species of algae score high on persistence. A freshwater algae *(Ulothrix)* is often used to illustrate the origin of gametes, i.e. the origin of sex-cells. The elongated filament-body of the algae generates a number of small spores which have lost the capacity to germinate (as they do in asexual reproduction): the spores come together and fuse to form a new individual – one of the simplest instances of the sex act.

Most primitive plant conjugation

As a precursor to more complex forms of bisexual reproduction a number of simple plant and animal species learned to "con-

Loose masses of fungal hyphae conjugate to form the cottony mycelium on mouldy bread.

jugate", i.e. to exchange genetic material between the individuals within a species in such a way that the offspring could be distinct from either parent. The classic example among plants is Pandorina, a 16-cell species: the cells are loosely attached and each has a pair of flagella, or protoplasmic whips, for the purpose of locomotion through the water. To reproduce, the cells separate and fuse with the similar cells from another floating colony. The common bread mould represents another instance of primitive plant conjugation. The mould grows in the form of a mass of microscopic threads collectively known as a mycelium. Threads of two different kinds come together to form a special type of spore in which a blending of genetic material has taken place. It may be fanciful to call the two kinds of threads, respectively, male and female, but this is a clear instance of early bisexual reproduction.

Earliest medium of sex cell transmission

One of the main problems in bisexual

reproduction is how to get the sex cells together. Or – looked at another way – the whole business of sex is so pleasurable for human beings that the main problem is to keep the sex cells apart, i.e. to achieve effective contraception. In its earliest stages biological evolution managed to contrive a variety of means whereby the "male" and "female" components could come together for reproduction: the penis and vagina arrangement was "late" in the evolutionary scale. The earliest species lived in water and simply released their sex cells – the earliest equivalents of "sperm" and "egg" – to float about. Some of the cells had cilia, moving hairs, to propel them along.

Most primitive hermaphrodite Siamese twins

This remarkable creature is a worm (*Diplozoon paradoxum* – the "paradoxical double animal"). It lives on the gills of carplike fish and as a hermaphrodite it is theoretically capable of mating with itself. In the course of maturing two of these parasitic worms grow together in the middle of their bodies and become effective Siamese twins joined together until death. The vagina of each half of the hermaphrodite becomes permanently linked to the sperm duct of the other half. William Bolsche termed the beast "a love monstrosity, an erotic Briareus with four sexual organs mating crosswise in a double marriage." There is more to the sex-life of worms than some of us realise!

Commonest instances of sex change

Birds start off with two embryological ovaries but in general only one – the left – develops to maturity and the right one remains rudimentary. If however the left ovary is destroyed by disease or deliberate experimental technique then the right ovary will develop, not into a mature ovary, but into a functional testis! In this way a complete sex reversal can occur in some species of domestic fowl. An erstwhile female may acquire cock plumage and tread and fertilize hens. There are instances on record where an individual started off by laying eggs and finished up fertilizing females. Sex reversal very rarely occurs in the opposite direction.

Most primitive sex change

Worms have a number of sexual tricks. In addition to exhibiting a range of heraphroditic abilities they can also undergo a complete sex reversal. Thus in one type of Syllis the female will change into a male once it has laid its eggs, and will then seek out a group of females to mate with. Females can be artificially converted into males by the simple expedient of cutting off half of the posterior ring of their bodies. (The ancient question that troubled the Greeks as to whether males or females enjoyed sex most could presumably be answered by worm individuals that have tried it both ways!) The oyster (*Ostea edulis*) also has the habit of changing sex, but with a frequency dependent upon temperature. In one study at 20-22°C., an individual became female once a year, where as at 14-16°C., once every three to four years!

Best known example of sex change

The wrasse – or Cleaner fish as it is known because of its habit of eating parasites from the skin, gills, and mouths of other fishes – is a brightly coloured fish living on Indo-Pacific coral reefs. In the words of the zoologist, R. Robertson (in "sex Changes under the Waves") – "The ultimate ambition of female Cleaner fish is to become male." A male generally dominates a group of females: if however he abandons his harem the most dominant of the remaining females begin to change sex within a few hours. The tendency in females towards sex change can be

The ultimate ambition of all female Wrasse fish is to become male.

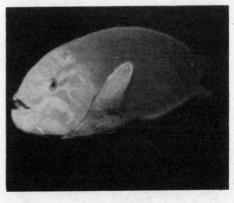

accounted for on the basis of an inspection of their gonads – the females are actually hermaphrodites as they all have small amounts of active (but walled-off) testicular material scattered through their ovaries. This peculiar situation among the wrasse is said to afford a number of ecological advantages.

Only instances of sex role reversal
The feminists derive little comfort from a glance at the animal world, where male and female roles are well defined and where the sexes conform to traditional moves of activity, i.e. males tend to be aggressive and dominant and females more interested in rearing the young. There are of course exceptions to this pattern. Female insects are often larger

Female sea-horses, unlike most animals, couldn't care less about traditional sex roles.

and more vicious than their husbands, and even among higher animals the "expected" sex roles do not always obtain. The female sea-horses actually possess a type of "penis", a prolonged genital papilla introduced into an opening in the male's abdominal sac. By this means the female introduces her eggs into a brood pouch in the male. Under this stimulation the male releases sperm into the pouch. The fertilized eggs develop, causing the abdomen of the "pregnant" father to swell enormously, until it is time for the male to give birth! Among birds the best known example of sex role reversal is the phalarope – the male sits on the eggs while the female goes out looking for food.

Most numerous sex organs in a species

As human beings we are accustomed to thinking of males having one penis and two testes and females having one vagina and two ovaries (though there are exceptions to this among men and women). However, a number of animals – generally quite primitive species – boast a greater quantity of sex organs. For instance the medusa of the water-living obelia, which looks like a tiny bell-shaped piece of clear jelly, has no less than four testes in the male and four ovaries in the female. Eggs and sperm are simply shed into the sea-water where fertilization takes place. But the most prolific number of sex organs can be found in our friend the tapeworm. It has been suggested that the tapeworm is "nothing but a bag of reproductive organs". In every segment there are bunches of testes and bunches of ovaries – which means that an individual adult can finish up with hundreds of gonads.

Largest penis in animal kingdom

It is appropriate that large animals should have large genital organs. The penis of the hippopotamus and elephant can be several feet in length, and uses have some-

"Are you still on about the one that got away?"

times been found for such weighty organs other than simple reproduction – the pizzle, for instance, formerly used for flogging, was in fact a bull's penis. Marshall's "Physiology of Reproduction" notes that the elephant penis is around 150 cm. in length, a third of which is formed by the pendulous portion. The biggest of all animal penises are to be found among the cetaceans, which include dolphins and whales. In large Rorqual whales the penis can be 10 ft. long with a diameter of up to 1 ft. The whale penis, at its base, consists of two arms attached to the pelvic bones; the arms fuse into the rope-like organ. The penis in cetaceans can generally be retracted into a penile slit.

Cetaceans (which include dolphins) have measurably the largest penises among animals.

Oddest penis

There is startling variation in the character of penises (penes) throughout the animal kingdom. Apart from size variation, already noted, shapes and colouring vary enormously. Insect and reptilian penises are often equipped with spines, corrugations, knobs, hooks, etc., to secure the female once insertion has taken place. If a copulating pair of insects or snakes are forcibly separated then either the male or the female may be irreparably damaged. The genital organs of the male may be torn off or the female may be terribly lacerated. Disengagement, following coitus, often needs to be a delicate business. The spines and hooks on certain animal penises are normal for the species and are often useful for purposes of classification. Sometimes however the penis may have congenital peculiarities that render coitus difficult if not impossible. One such instance is the "Corkscrew Penis" in bulls. Here the penis springs into a spiral just prior to coitus, preventing access to the cow. Veterinary experts do not seem at all clear as to why this condition occurs.

Fastest erection

In many mammalian males the speed of erection is remarkably fast. A period of three or four seconds from a fully flaccid state to full erection is commonplace and in many species the time is even less than this. Kinsey has remarked that "stallions, bulls, rams, rats, guinea pigs, porcupines, cats, dogs, apes, and males of other species may come to full erection almost instantaneously upon contact with a sexual object." As we may expect, the youngest men get the speediest erections in humans.

Most copious ejaculators

Whales, as may be expected, generate the greatest volume of seminal discharge – and the substance is sometimes discernable in the sea after a male has ejaculated. Among domesticated mammals the boar is usually cited as producing the greatest volume of ejaculate. The volume of fluid averages around 200 ml, but the range is from 100 ml to 500 ml (the upper limit representing a generous cupful). The volume of ejaculate in domestic animals has been monitored for purposes of artificial insemination. The artificial vagina for A.I. practices began development in the early thirties and is associated with the names of Milovanov (1932) and Rodolfo (1934)

Semen volume varies enormously between species – whales, as might be expected, come out on top.

Largest mammalian litter
The largest mammalian litter ever recorded at a single birth is 36, in the case of the common tenrec *(Centetes ecaudatus)* found in Madagascar and the Comoro Islands. Most litters number about 14.

Most convincing female orgasm

There has been considerable debate as to whether female animals experience orgasm. Bronowski, for instance has been prepared to declare that the human female is the only animal to experience orgasm. There is some inconclusive evidence that hermaphrodite snails can experience orgasm (e.g. rising curves of electrical excitement followed by discharge), and some evidence also that female rabbits experience orgasm. This question intrigued Kinsey and he wrote to various researchers who were supposed to know all about rabbits. Klein, for instance, wrote to Kinsey – "... I have very often observed a quite definite peak of response with climax, from which the female falls back abruptly into a quiet state. ..." Hammond too believed there was orgasm in female rabbits and female ferrets (with regard to the latter he wrote – "A film of copulation in the ferret would, I think, show you by the expression on the face of the female that an orgasm did occur.")

Largest participants in group sex

It will come as no surprise to those interested in the animal world as a whole that human beings did not invent the idea

Small surprise that whales rate high in a number of sexual superlatives (see below).

of group sexual activity. Arthropods, for example, frequently engage in such practices, as do various more highly developed species. Cetaceans – porpoises, for example – are particularly keen on various group sex activities, and so are their larger brothers and sisters, the whales. Of Grey Whales H. Wendt noted in "The Sex Life of Animals": – "Another interesting habit is that mating is done in three's, one female and two males. The role of the second male is not well understood but it has something to do with mutual assistance." When we think of the size of these creatures perhaps we begin to appreciate why some "mutual assistance" in mating is required.

Most primitive kissers

Roman snails are very keen on sex play prior to copulation. The preliminary courting can include extensive rocking to and fro, rearing up, and rhythmic oscillations. The sex play can also include what Wendt has termed "smacking kisses". After all these happy preliminaries the actual copulation itself may last for several minutes.

Longest kissers

Many fish appear to take pleasure in kissing: this is particularly the case with "ornamental" fish. Wendt remarks that "The couples use their lips in the ceremonies of courtship in a surprisingly human manner." One particular type of labyrinth fish is known as the "kissing gurami". In this species the enthusiasm for the kiss is such that one such act may last as much as twenty-five minutes. Doubtless human kisses can exceed this duration but such achievements must be rare.

First virgin birth amongst domestic fowl

Birds and mammals are not known to have produced parthenogenetic populations in the wild. But, oddly enough, experimenters working with turkeys have had considerable success in producing parthenogenetic strains. Using more than 42,000 eggs American scientists were able to increase the number of eggs "which started to develop" from 16.7 per cent in 1952 to 41.7 per cent in 1959. This improvement was a result of selective breeding. Birds producing a high proportion of eggs with parthenogenetic tendencies were mated from males descended from other such birds. Towards the end of the experiment 67 embryos were reared to hatching, a few survived to maturity, three produced sperm, and one actually produced off-

Above: A kissing gourami – the act may last as long as twenty-five minutes.

spring. More recently, Patricia Sarvella of the US Department of Agriculture reported the birth of four male parthenogenetic chickens, hatched from 8,532 eggs: all four reached maturity ("Nature", vol. 243, p.171).

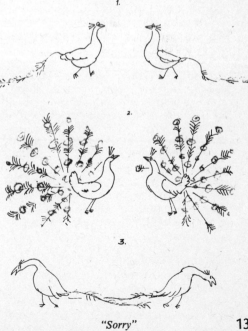

"Sorry"

Least expected masturbatory activity

Most of us tend to associate masturbatory activities with the genitals, though a few of us may also think of such bodily parts as the nipples or anus. It is curious that the antlers of deer are also an extremely effective masturbatory tool. It appears that during the rutting season – generally between September and October – the hardened antlers constitute a highly sensitive erotic zone. Darling has been quoted ("A Herd of Red Deer") – masturbation "is accomplished by lowering the head and gently drawing the tips of the antlers to and fro through the herbage. Erection and extrusion of the penis from the sheath follow in five to seven seconds ... Ejaculation follows about five seconds after the penis is erected ... These antlers, used now so delicately, may within a few minutes be used with all the body's force behind them to clash with the antlers of another stag."

First animal love songs

Many animals produce mating-calls and more complex sequences of sounds that may be termed "love-songs." Insects, for instance, generate involved musical sequences and many water-living crea-

A red deer with absolutely no doubts about what to do with his antlers (see left).

tures produce sounds, some of which are outside the range of human hearing. Amphibians first produced love-songs that could have been heard by human beings – had there been any alive at the time. Amphibians first started singing to each other on dry land, somewhere between two hundred and three hundred and fifty million years ago, in the Carboniferous Period. Thus Wendt – "... we can scarcely imagine that the as yet unknown ancestors of frogs who lived in the earlier Paleozoic Era did not jump and croak. How otherwise would they have met for mating?" Perhaps the argument is not conclusive but it is oddly romantic to think of animals first beginning to communicate by sound.

Longest love songs

Many animals communicate to each other, generally for purposes of mating, with long complex sound sequences. Each sound sequence – in birds, insects, etc. – may legitimately be termed a song, and what is surprising is the complexity of some of these compositions. Whales, for

example, can "sing" to each other over vast distances – up to a hundred miles, the water carrying the great booming sounds. And a single sound-sequence, i.e. a song, can last for as long as thirty minutes without repetition. We are accustomed to whales breaking anatomical records in the animal kingdom. Perhaps we would less quickly think of them as proficient songsters.

Most complex insect love songs
Among grasshoppers the *Saltatoria* emit "complex and highly specific songs." The hind legs are rubbed against the wings and the sounds produced are perceived by tympanal organs on the legs. Such activity is a clear mating display. Above a certain temperature the males of the species may

sing spontaneously, sounding a number of notes followed by a pause. A receptive female answers with a softer call. The male and female then call alternately, the male now with a newly modified song. In threat displays two males may sing at each other. Perdeck has shown ("The Isolating Value of Specific Song Patterns in Two Sibling Species of Grasshoppers – *Chorthippus brunneus* Thumb and *C. biggutulus* L." "Behaviour", Vol. 12, pp. 1-75) that grasshopper songs are sexually stimulating to both sexes. In fact females get so excited that they even try to mate with silent males of the wrong species; and males speed up their locomotion and their efforts to copulate.

Most vaginas in one animal
Most animals needing a vagina make do with one. Some animals – by accident or intention – finish up with two. In the duckbill, the spiny anteater (i.e. in the *monotremes*), and in the marsupials the vaginas are paired, as are various other bits and pieces in the female genital arrangement. In the embryo the uterine tube, uterus and vagina exist as paired and entirely separate structures – and so they remain in adults of the species mentioned: This "paired" feature – common to some animals can appear as an abnormality, prohibiting reproduction, in others. Where there is a congenital fault a female may be born with a double uterus and inadequate channels to a double or single vagina. In humans surgery can be attempted.

Most unusual mammalian vagina
Most mammalian vaginas are more or less the same in overall configuration: they basically comprise a smoothish lubricated channel to allow penile insertion and subsequent parturition. Some vaginas are however exceptional. One such is the vagina in the female hippopotamus, coming equipped as it does with 10 to 19 transverse interlocking fibrous ridges. The ridges at the upper end of the vagina are the most pronounced, resembling heavy corrugations. Similar, though less pronounced, corrugations are discernible in the vagina of pig and warthog. In all cases the function of the ridges is a mystery.

Longest clitoris

The clitoris of the female whale is about 8 cm. long. Its apex is said to be "triloped" and is directed backwards. The whale clitoris, in common with the other sex organs of the largest cetaceans, are the biggest of any animal. Many other species have organs large for their body size, and in a number of species there is a long clitoris. We have already noted the large clitoris in the hyaena and the spider monkey. It is also surprisingly long in the mole (in the non-breeding season it is as long as the penis). In cats and civets the clitoris is a complicated structure reinforced with bone, and the organ is particularly prominent. Considering the absence of any functional role for the clitoris in most species it is a surprisingly impressive device in many species.

In common with the genital features of a wide range of species the clitoris is sometimes paired in a female animal. Or, put another way, the clitoris appears in two halves. Sometimes only part of the clitoris is paired, i.e. it branches towards the upper end. In marsupials the *glans clitoridis* frequently appears as a paired organ. In some reptiles a similar phenomenon can be observed in the penis but female reptiles possess no clitoris whatsoever – this does not seem to detract from enjoyment of coitus!

Largest mammary glands

Back to whales again! In general, cetaceans have no protruding udders like cows. Whale mammaries are two long and fairly flat organs inclined to each other at a slight angle. Their tips are not far from the umbilicus, and the average dimensions in "resting" Rorqual cows are about 7 ft. by 2 ft. 6 in. by $2\frac{1}{4}$ in. In lactation, as with all other mammals, there are discernible changes in the size of the mammary glands. During lactation, the thickness of the glands can increase from as little as the $2\frac{1}{4}$ in. mentioned to a maximum of 1 ft.: and the colour changes from pink to golden brown. If the glands are strongly distended, the nipples can be detected from the outside. Jets of milk have been seen to shoot from the nipples of whale carcasses, when whalers call them "milk-filled" – a sure sign that the animal was lactating.

Most coital thrusts by howler monkeys

Why howler monkeys, you may well ask? I have no excuse except that when I came across the superlative it seemed quite intriguing. Doubtless some monkeys have achieved a greater number of penile thrusts, but if they have I do not know of them. In one set of observations a male howler monkey managed no less than

Howler monkeys in the wild have attracted the most bizarre sexual research.

twenty-eight penile thrusts in a single intromission, after which period we may deduce that climax occurred or the fellow got bored.

Least coital thrusts by howler monkeys

In the same set of observations as those mentioned above the minimum number of thrusts was also noted – and turned out to be eight. I rather suspect that human records would be more impressive, with possibly several hundred thrusts before climax in certain instances and only one or two in others. But in fairness it must be admitted that the performance of the various primates has hardly been examined in any detail in this respect. There may well be sturdier howler monkeys than the ones observed!

Longest sperm

Sperm come in a wide variety of shapes but in general tend to be elongated, to resemble simple filaments. The sperm of crayfish are star-shaped, while some have undulating membranes, explosive capsules, etc. It has been said that sperm never exceed 50 microns (1 micron=1 thousandth of a millimetre) in diameter, but there are a number of species in which the sperm attain remarkable lengths. In amphibia of the family *Discoglossidae*

sperm can sometimes be as much as 2.mm in length, and in the aquatic *Notonecta* the staggering length of 12 mm. is attained! Perhaps even more remarkable is the fact that in the ostracods, minute crustaceans, the sperm are six times as long as the entire body of the animal! When they are generated they are curled up in compact form.

Longest vagina

The vagina in the largest species is, by the standards of mere mortals, an extraordinarily capacious device. Elephants do not have the biggest vaginas but they are quite impressive in the magnitude of their genital apparatus. In the female elephant the vagina is a "simple, capacious tube which measures nearly 50 cm. in length." We may expect this channel to expand considerably upon insertion of the male organ. It is of some interest that the female genital channel comes equipped with a large transversely placed hymen. The largest vagina in the animal kingdom is unquestionably that of the whale. This need hardly surprise us as the female whale has to accommodate the largest animal penis. In the words of one writer (Marshall's "Physiology of Reproduction, 1," 1, p.99) "the vulva is a long elliptical groove which lies immediately cranial to the anus." The longest whale vagina is in the order of 6 to 8 ft. in length, capable of further elongation if necessary upon penile insertion.

"I miss the children"

Most nipples

It is estimated that breast-feeding began more than 200 million years ago, the time of the first mammals (Which laid eggs and hatched them). Subsequently no less than 18,000 different species of mammals evolved. The kangaroo has the unique ability to produce two types of milk from two teats for young of different ages. It is curious that the number of teats or nipples varies throughout the mammalian world. The horse and elephant, for instance, have only two nipples; and though the cow has only one udder the single massive gland empties into four teats. The dog has five paired glands. The hog can have as many as eighteen mammae. Supernumerary nipples are common in many species, e.g. primates, rodents, ruminants. The largest number of nipples is present in *Centetes,* a primitive insectivore with twenty-two to twenty-four nipples and as many as thirty-six young at birth.

Largest animal testes

It will hardly come as a surprise that elephants and whales have big testes: these creatures are after all weighty fellows. In one adult elephant the two testes weighted 1.8 kg. and 2.2 kg. respectively, and the left one measured 175mm. x 150mm. x 115mm. in length, width, and thickness. It has been noted that bladder urine collected as much as twelve hours after death contained a large number of motile sperm. The really massive testes however belong to whales. On the whale the testes are only visible when the abdominal cavity has been opened and the intestines removed or pushed aside: the testes are two fairly elongated cylindrical organs with a white, smooth, and shiny surface. As has been pointed out, even when the whale testes have been located they are hard to handle since they weigh 60, 15, and 25 lb. in Fin, Sei, and Sperm whales respectively. In Blue Whales the testes may be more than two feet six inches long and weigh up to 100 lb, each!

Longest mammalian intercourse

Coitus of the longest duration in mammals occurs in mink and sable. Unlike coitus in other species, there is no "locking" of the genitals, but when intromission has once been achieved it is maintained for very long periods: several ejaculations can occur with rests between them. Timed matings of the sable have lasted for as long as 8 hours from the moment of original insertion until the time of withdrawal. One authority (Marshall's "Physiology of Reproduction") gives coitus in the mink, as in the ferret, as "prolonged" and usually lasting for 30 to 40 minutes – with a range of 20 minutes to 2 hours. Ovulation follows after a period of about 40 hours: if conception does not occur, the animal experiences a state of "pseudo-pregnancy."

Longest coital session

As in all other matters sexual there is immense variation throughout the animal kingdom in the actual duration of the coital act. In fact intercourse can range from a few seconds to many hours. Copulating snakes typically remain in union for one or two hours or for much longer periods – there is a suggestion that six to twelve hours is average. The record is held by a pair of rattlesnakes who remained in copulatory connection for no less than 22¾ hours. Such long periods may in part be explained by the difficulty the male has, on account of his spiked penis, in getting away! The fluke, *Schistosoma heamatobium* – with the female eternally living within a fissure in the male's body – has been said to exist in a state of "permanent copulation."

Shortest coital session

We have already seen that chimps do not take very long over coitus; a number of other mammals are even swifter. Slijper has noted that bulls, rams, and stags copulate "with astonishing rapidity" and that the whole process lasts no more than

Huge African bull elephant. One's testes weighed nearly five pounds each.

a few seconds. Horses manage a few minutes. Whales too are said to copulate very rapidly, a circumstance no doubt conditioned by their ungainly mass. In some descriptions of whale coitus the great beasts are said to dive, then to swim towards each other at great speed, "then to surface vertically and to copulate belly to belly." In this act it is often the case that the entire thorax and part of the abdomen protrudes out of the water. Slijper reports eye-witness accounts of such whale copulations. Horizontal copulations in whales is also described, a mode allowing coitus to last up to 30 seconds.

Shortest coital session amongst insects

Insects, we noted, achieve the longest genital coitus. They are versatile enough, in other species, to manage the shortest also. Many insects mate on the wing, allowing only a second or two of contact. As one example, various types of mosquitoes perform a sex act that lasts only 2 or 3 seconds.

141

Most sexually active sheep

Many species of sheep only breed once a year. Hampshire Down sheep are traditionally given access to rams in the summer and do not, as a rule, breed more than once. Many foreign breeds of sheep, however, lamb twice a year, e.g. the horned sheep which run half-wild in Patani in the Malay Peninsula. Indigenous sheep of India are said to produce lambs three times in two years, and there is no definite season for lambing. In Argentina the merinos have two annual breeding seasons within the year, but it has been suggested that this may only represent a single, though extensive breeding season. The highest degree of sexual activity experienced by any sheep is shown by certain Australian merinos, which can breed through the year – which implies, in the absence of gestation, an unbroken series of oestrous cycles. A report of the Chief Inspector of Stock for New South Wales (1891) has been quoted as dividing the time of lambing into six periods which embrace the entire year.

Nymphomania first induced in cattle

This frightening condition was first induced in cattle by the careful administering of chemicals. Pellet implantation resulted in continuous oestrogen administration with resulting changes in the sexual enthusiasm and receptivity of cattle.

Most sexually adventurous

It is a feature of most copulating species that they copulate the same way each time. A few diligent researchers have observed monkeys and apes copulating face-to-face, an uncommon position for non-human primates – but in general there is little or no variation in basic coital position. Insects of different species, however, mate in many different ways. The male may effectively lie along the female, or the female may be uppermost. In some insect copulations one partner may be above but the genitals may curve under and make contact from *beneath* the other partner. In yet other instances the two insects may lie in opposite directions with only the genital region in contact.

Most vicious form of intercourse

A number of female insects eat their husbands during the coital act. It has been argued that in the praying mantis, for example, the male can only copulate successfully when half his head has been eaten away – something to do with releasing nervous inhibitions! It has been pointed out that mantises will mate satisfactorily in the terrarium if the female's terrible forelimbs are tied before she is introduced to the male – so perhaps cannibalism is not essential to coitus. The females among many insect-eating *Diptera* are also apt to gnaw away at their husbands, and a variety of other fates may await the amorous male. In the fly *Serromyia femorata,* of the family *Ceratopogonidae,* mating takes place with the two ventral surfaces together and the mouthparts touching. At the end of mating, the female sucks out the body content of the male through the mouth. In the *Asilidae,* the male sometimes eats the female during or after mating.

Most remarkable coital mechanics

We have already noted some rather surprising preliminaries or accompaniments to insect coitus, but the mechanics of the coital act itself is sometimes equally remarkable. In bed bug copulation the sperm is placed in a pocket in the cuticle on the ventral surface of the female abdomen, whereupon the sperm actually makes its way through the body wall and reaches the ovaries via the blood stream. In many species – some bed bugs (as well as leeches, planarians, etc.) – the penis actually penetrates the body wall, resulting in a form of hypodermic insemination.

On account of his size, the male mantis doesn't stand a chance!

Part VI

Contraception & Castration

Most optimistic method

This form of coital activity, involving withdrawal of the penis so that no semen is ejaculated into the vagina, has long been practiced as an optimistic contraceptive method. The famous biblical example is to be found in Genesis XXXVIII, 8-10 – "And Judah said unto Onan, Go in unto thy brother's wife, and marry her, and raise up seed to thy brother. And Onan knew that the seed should not be his and it came to pass, when he went in unto his brother's wife, that he spilled it on the ground, lest that he should give seed to his brother. And the thing which he did displeased the Lord; wherefore he slew him also." God's hasty action, seemingly commonplace in those days, has been taken by the Church as a justification for all manner of obscurantism in the fields of masturbation and contraception.

First recommendation of coitus reservatus

Coitus reservatus, whereby a man puts his penis inside a woman's vagina but aims not to ejaculate, has been practiced for a variety of religious, moral, contraceptive and other reasons. According to one authority it was first advocated by Dr Alice Stockham of Chicago at the end of the nineteenth century, and later by Dr Marie Stopes. Stockham can be quoted – "Manifestations of tenderness are indulged in without physical or mental fatigue; the caresses lead up to connection (coupling) and the sexes unite quietly and closely. Once the necessary control has been acquired, the two beings are fused and reach sublime spiritual joy. This union can be accompanied by slow controlled motions, so that voluptuous thrills do not overbalance the desire for soft sensations. If there is no wish to procreate, the violence of the orgasm will thus be avoided. If love is mutual, and if union is sufficiently prolonged, it affords complete satisfaction without emission or orgasm. After an hour the bodies relax, spiritual delight is increased, and new horizons are revealed with the renewal of strength." When Dr Stockham's book first appeared it was condemned by medical men in Britain and America. In more recent times some sexologists approve the method espoused; others condemn it. For instance, Dr Robert Chartham urges that

"it is *not* a method of lovemaking to be recommended..."

Most ridiculous methods

Soranus (A.D. 98-138) was a Greek physician who studied in Alexandria and later practised in Rome under Hadrian. He found enough time to write forty books or so. In his "Gynaecology" he suggests – "...that a woman ought, in the moment during coitus when the man ejaculates his sperm, to hold her breath, draw her body back a little so that the semen cannot penetrate into the *os uteri,* then immediately get up and sit down with bent knees, and in this position, provoke sneezes" (quoted by S. Green, "The Curious History".) Thus, it is hoped, she will avoid conception.

Most bizarre methods of contraception

Many of the most bizarre contraceptive measures date from antiquity and involve magical practices and gross superstition. Many odd recommendations can also be found in modern times. William Godwin, for instance, in the early nineteenth-century, was not averse to a bit of infanticide (hardly contraceptive but at any rate a form of family planning). He remarked – "if the alternative were complete, I had rather such a child should perish in the first hour of its existence, than that a man should spend seventy years of life in a state of misery and vice". In 1838 the idea of systematic infanticide was put forward in all seriousness by another man calling himself "Marcus." In this man's view all babies after the third born into a poor family should be killed during their first sleep by mixing a deadly gas with the air they were breathing. Less drastically, in 1806, Thomas Ewell suggested that couples only copulate in "vessels filled with carbonic acid or azotic gas." This on the grounds that "coition will always be unfruitful unless it be done in pure air." Weinhold recommended the infibulation of poor men, invalids, servants, apprentices, etc. – until they found themselves capable of supporting a wife and children. Noyes and others suggested *coitus reservatus* as an effective contraceptive measure.

AD 1550

• JUGOSLAVIJA — POLENŠAK

BEFORE GOING TO THE MARRIAGE CEREMONY THE BRIDE PUT AN UNLOCKED PADLOCK INTO THE BODICE OF HER DRESS. SHE DECIDED UPON THE NUMBER OF HER CHILDLESS YEARS BY MAKING THE SAME NUMBER OF STEPS OUTSIDE HER HOUSE WITH THE PADLOCK UNLOCKED, THEN SHE LOCKED IT.

AD 1600

• JUGOSLAVIJA — PAVLOVCI AT ORMOŽ

WHEN THE BRIDE—GROOM CAME TO TAKE THE BRIDE TO THE MARRIAGE CEREMONY, SHE CLIMBED UP A LADDER AS MANY RUNGS AS SHE WANTED TO HAVE CHILDREN IN HER WEDLOCK.

AD 1650

• JUGOSLAVIJA — ČRNI VRH ABOVE IDRIJA

WOMEN REMAINED CHILDLESS THE SAME NUMBER OF YEARS AS WAS THAT OF THE BARLEY GRAINS THROWN INTO THEIR WEDDING SHOES.

147

Earliest contraceptives

Fragments of Egyptian papyri, found at Kahun in El Faiyūm in 1889, are the oldest medical literature that has come down to us from antiquity. They reveal that upper class Egyptian women of the Twelfth Dynasty, about 1850 B.C., used crocodile dung as a pessary, irrigated the vagina with honey and natron (native sesquicarbonate of soda), and inserted a gum-like substance in the vagina. Though elephant's dung was later substituted for that of the crocodile, a similar prescription was used in various places for some three thousand years. It is likely that the contraceptive measures had some effect. Honey and gum would clog the motile sperm; and crocodile's dung, slightly alkaline, would not be much different from a spermicide carried in a sponge. The Ebers papyrus (about 1550 B.C.) contained a prescription for the use of lint tampons moistened with juice from fermented tips of acacia shrubs, i.e. lactic acid.

First propagandist to be jailed

Charles Knowlton, born in 1800 in Massachusetts, became the first man in history to go to jail for advocating birth control. He was a self-taught freethinker who never left New England, except for two brief visits to New York State. In 1832 he published a birth control classic, "Fruits of Philosophy, or the Private Companion of Young Married People"; and the work helped to establish him as the founder of American contraceptive medicine. At the time the value of "Fruits of Philosophy" were not noticed. The "Boston Medical and Surgical Journal" primly talked of the "unnatural measures" proposed, adding that "the less that is known about it by the public at large, the better it will be for the morals of the community." Three sets of prosecutions were launched against Knowlton, one resulting in a fifty dollar fine and costs, another in three months hard labour in a house of correction.

First propagandist in U.K.

Francis Place, born in Drury Lane in 1771, began the birth control movement in Britain in 1823. After immense early struggles he managed to become a prosperous tradesman, expressing the ambition that he would retire at forty-five and devote himself to politics. His commitment to birth control was only one facet of his deep social and political involvement in reformist philosophy on several fronts.

First female propagandist in U.S.

If Knowlton was the first male propagandist for birth control in America, then Margaret Sanger was the first woman to be active in the same field. Her role in America has been compared to that of Marie Stopes in Britain. Mrs. Sanger was a declared socialist and took part in the various activities of the Labour movement. She marched with the "Wobblies" (The Industrial Workers of the World), and in 1914 began to publish a magazine called "The Woman Rebel," determined to make it as "red and flaming as possible." Apart from the "Rebel," Mrs. Sanger produced a small pamphlet called "Family Limitation".

Margaret Sanger

It was soon announced that Mrs. Sanger had violated nine federal statutes; and under the Comstock regime, the man whose organisation, the New York Society for the Suppression of Vice made merry war against contraceptionists, she was prosecuted. She fled to England the day before the trial was due to be held. She met Marie Stopes and is said to have fallen in love with Havelock Ellis. Later she returned to America and lived through many tumultuous events.

First Family Planning clinic

The first birth control clinic in the world was opened in Holland in 1882 under the auspices of the *Nieuw Malthusiaanschen Bond* (the Dutch Malthusian League). The League was founded in 1881 – and was immediately opposed by the medical profession! Two doctors, however, joined the organization in the early days – Dr. de Rooy (1881) and Dr. Aletta Jacobs (1882), the first woman to become medically qualified in Holland. From 1883 Dr. Jacobs

held a clinic twice a week to give advice on infant welfare to working-class women. Soon she became aware of the Mensinga Diaphragm and started giving birth control advice.

Dr. Aletta Jacobs

Marie Stopes, blighted by an upbringing so puritanical that it took her three years to realize that her husband was impotent.

First Family Planning clinic in U.K.

The first birth control clinic in Britain was opened by Marie Stopes and her husband in Holloway on 17 March 1921. A framed inscription on the wall of the clinic ran as follows –

This, the first Birth Control Clinic in the British Empire, was opened on the 17 March 1921, by Humphrey Verdon Roe and his wife Marie Carmichael Stopes, in order to show by actual example what might be done for mothers and their children with no great difficulty, and what should be done all over the world when once the idea takes root in the public mind that motherhood should be voluntary and guided by the best scientific knowledge available.

The clinic is free to all, and is supported entirely by the two founders. Those who have benefited by its help are asked to hand on a knowledge of its existence to others and help to create a public opinion which will force the Ministry of Health to include a similar service in Ante-Natal and Welfare Centres already supported by the Government in every district.

First F.P. Association in U.K.

The British Family Planning Association was founded in 1930 on a voluntary basis. A number of other countries had already set up similar organizations.

First F.P. Association in U.S.

The first Family Planning Association on the American continent was created in 1917, despite the lingering influence of Comstock, hostile contraceptive legislation in many states, etc.

First F.P. Association in South Africa

South Africa, perhaps not the most liberal of countries managed to get a Family Planning Association started in 1932. Today the government provides a variety of family planning services.

First F.P. Association in Australia

The Australian Family Planning Association was started in 1926, four years before the creation of a similar body in the UK. As with other FPAs, the Australian organization was on a voluntary basis.

Most famous hoax

A Canadian doctor, a certain J. S. Greenstein, published a paper on a wholly fictitious contraceptive which he called "Armpitin," for which he sketched the chemical formula, including several molecular groups represented by the initials NO. "Armpitin," he explained, was found to affect males by way of the olfactory nerve, and rendered them sterile for a number of days equivalent to the number of NO groups in the formula. The paper was seriously reviewed in an annual review of pharmacology, and Dr. Greenstein received requests from pharmaceutical companies to sell them the patent.

Highest estimates of failure rates
Various figures have been given for failure rates for contraceptive measures of various sorts. Highest estimates have been quoted as follows (figures for pregnancies/100 woman-years of exposure):

pill	2.0
condom	11.1
diaphragm and jelly	17.5
withdrawal	20.0
safe period	35.0
foaming tablets, douching	42.8

Lowest estimates of failure rates
Lowest estimates for contraceptive measures of various types are as follows (figures for pregnancies/100 woman-years of exposure):

pill	0.1
condom	7.5
diaphragm and jelly	7.2
withdrawal	12.0
safe period	14.4
foaming tablets, douching	11.9

According to one estimate, the least popular methods of contraception in Britain are the coil/IUD (used by five per cent of married couples), spermicides (five per cent), rhythm method/safe period (six per cent), and the cap/diaphragm with spermicidal cream or jelly (six per cent).

Pessaries first marketed
The chemist W. J. Rendell began making up quinine and cacao-butter pessaries in about 1880, which he distributed among the poor who lived around the Clerkenwell area of London, where his shop was situated. The demand soon became so great that producing the suppositories became a full time job. Rendell, in common with many of the conception pioneers in the nineteenth-century, was a convinced freethinker: when he advertised himself in Bradlaugh's National Reformer in 1885 he styled himself "M.N.S.S." (member of the National Secular Society).

CONDOM
First used
Hercules Saxonia recalled, in 1597, that Fallopius had invented the linen condom, and further suggested that it could be improved by soaking it in a chemical solution several times and allowing it to dry in the shade. While it is conceded that Fallopius was one of the first to mention the sheath or condom it is also stressed that such a device was probably invented in many different parts of the world at different times. It is possible that sheaths of various types were used in ancient Rome – there is a legend, related by Antoninus Liberalis, of a goat's bladder being employed as a female sheath. According to the tale, Minos, the King of Crete, had a problem – his semen contained serpents and scorpions which injured the women with whom he made love. Happily his wife Pasiphae was immune to the creatures, yet the union was sterile. A remedy was discovered when a goat's bladder was placed in the vagina of a second woman. Minos ejaculated his serpents into this obliging lady and then could cohabit with Pasiphae who thereupon conceived. Sheaths could also have been used in ancient times for decoration as well as for contraception.

There is an illustration of an Egyptian wearing a sheath that hangs in clumsy fashion before him. And it has been suggested that use of the condom in ancient Egypt could well date to the XIX Dynasty (1350 B.C. to 1200 B.C.).

151

First invented

In 1564 the "De Morbo Gallico" of Gabriello Fallopio (1523-1563) was published posthumously. Here the Italian anatomist described the linen sheath he claimed to have invented. Made to fit the glans of the penis it was devised essentially as a protective against venereal disease. The foreskin had to be pulled over the device to keep it in place. An alternative

Casanova, one of the first men to use condoms as contraception rather than to prevent VD, seems never to have sired a child.

usage suggested by Fallopius must have been even more difficult – to insert the sheath in the urethra. He did claim however to have tested the sheath on 1,100 men, with not one of them becoming infected.

The word first used

There has been immense debate about the origin of the word *condom*. One suggestion was that there was a Dr. (or Colonel) Condom (or Condum, Condon, or Conton) – a physician at the court of Charles II – who invented the device. The word first appeared in print in a poem written in 1706 – "A Scots Answer to a British Vision," which refers to contemporary instruments for combating venereal disease (*Sirenge and Condum/Come both in Request*).

First used in France

It is certain that the glans sheath was used in Paris as early as 1655. French sources also refer to a number of contraceptive alternatives of that time, including withdrawal. Not everyone was enthusiastic about the new invention. Madame de Sévigné described the condom as "armour against enjoyment and a spider web against danger."

Madame de Sévigné

First used in England

The condom was probably first used in England, as in much of the rest of Europe, in the seventeenth-century. A witness before the first English Birthrate Commission testified that condoms were in use in London at the time of the Great Fire (1666).

Earliest manufacture of modern condom

The historical condoms must have been unreliable to a marked degree, simply because of difficulties in manufacture. Developments in rubber technology in the nineteenth century allowed, for the first time, the standardized production of improved contraceptive sheaths. Of particular relevance was the vulcanization process, first carried out in 1843.

ORAL
First

Following the work of Chang and Djerassi and others, Gregory Pincus, the Director of the Worcester Foundation for Experimental Biology had developed an effective contraceptive pill by 1957. The Pincus team, including Chang, began a systematic study, in the nineteen-fifties, of more than two hundred substances with varying effects on such things as ovulation, menstruation, and conception. One substance, gestagen type, called "norethynodrel," formed the basis of the first large-scale trial of the contraceptive pill, a trial carried out in Puerto Rico in 1956. The gestagens, however, gave poor control over menstruation, a problem overcome by combining the gestagen with a synthetic oestrogen. It was a combined pill of this type (marketed commercially as Enovid) that proved so successful in the Puerto Rican trial. Now there are literally dozens of contraceptive pills available. **153**

Most bizarre suggested consequences

Many strange occurrences have been laid at the door of the pill. Sometimes there are good grounds for thinking that oral contraception can have very strange effects on some women. One patient complained that whenever she turned over in bed, or sneezed, she could feel and hear something crackling in her chest. It transpired that her breastbone was loose – the doctor advised her to go off the pill! A Manchester dentist found that a patient with loose teeth was on the pill. One particularly bizarre finding was that women who were taking the pill were supplying green (!) blood plasma to the Leeds Regional Blood Transfusion Centre in 1968. A case described in the "British Medical Journal" indicated that the pill might be able to cause the equivalent of St. Vitus's Dance.

Most persistent British critic

The most persistent critic of the pill in Britain has been the Australian-born specialist in human metabolism, Professor Victor Wynn, head of the Alexander Simpson Laboratory for Metabolic Research at St. Mary's Hospital, London. His concern over the subject grew out of his study of the pill's effects on how the body handles carbohydrates, and on the pattern of blood fats in women. His studies in this area have been extensive.

First relevant to Court damages

A rich market for the pill manufacturers is Australasia, where around one million women "contracept orally" – a figure that represents more than one third of the women of childbearing age. The pill is coming to be regarded as one of a woman's natural entitlements. In November 1969 a news sheet was circulated amongst British drug firms stating that a Melbourne bride-to-be, who had hurt her leg in a car crash, had been awarded £230 by a court, because the risk of thrombosis probably meant she would never be able to take the pill!

STERILIZATION
First committee recommendation for mental defectives

In 1934 a Departmental Committee on Sterilization, known as the Brock Committee, recommended unanimously that sterilization be made legal for mental defectives, those suffering from, or believed likely to transmit, mental disease, and persons suffering from or believed to be carriers of grave physical disabilities which had been shown to be transmissible. The recommendations referred only to the *right* of such people to be sterilized and required the consent of the person to the operation. But if the person was a minor, or "incapable," then the guardian could give permission for the operation to be performed. The question has been asked – who is the guardian of a mental defective or lunatic in a public institution? An official of the state! The Brock Committee's report was never adopted.

First proposed on eugenic grounds

The earliest published recommendation of sterilization on eugenic grounds is that of a Swiss, Dr. August Forel, in 1892. It was such early agitation that led up to the European enthusiasm for sterilization in the nineteen-thirties.

VASECTOMY
First on animals

The first recorded animal vasectomy, in this case the tying of the *vas deferens* in a dog, occurred in 1823. Sir Astley Cooper Bart, F.R.S. (1768-1848), who had experimental surgery as a hobby, wrote –

In 1823 I made the following experiment on a dog. I divided the *vas deferens* on one side and the spermatic artery and vein on the other.

"And remember to call in for a vasectomy on your way home"

In 1829 I killed him, and found the *vas deferens* below the division excessively enlarged and full of semen (sic), and entirely stopped, with some separation of its extremities; but it was open from the place of division to the urethra.

The testis upon that side on which the artery and vein were divided gangrened and sloughed away . . .

The testis on the side on which the duct was divided became somewhat larger than natural. I kept the dog for six years; during that time he was twice seen *in coitu,* but the female did not produce. This was in 1827.

First on humans

Maurice Meltzer, writing in 1928, has declared that four men – Guyon, Burket, Hilton, and Harrison – performed vasectomies between 1885 and 1896; but doubt has been expressed about this claim. Guyon wrote of his experiences with "resection of the vasa deferentia" in 1895 and it is clear that Isnardi performed vasectomies in 1896, but the first human vasectomies were performed either by Harrison in London (possibly as early as 1893) or by Lennander in Uppsala, Sweden (in 1894).

First used as treatment for criminals

In 1899, Dr. Harry C. Sharp, as medical officer of the Jefferson Reformatory in Indiana, performed the first vasectomy as treatment for a "criminal," i.e. a compulsive masturbator. A young man of nineteen called Clawson, greatly worried by his masturbatory habits, approached Dr. Sharp to request castration. Even in 1899 no sane doctor would have granted such a request. Dr. Sharp remarked, forty years later, "I did not feel justified in performing that mutilation." However, he did think that a vasectomy would help; and on the 12th October 1899 Clawson was sterilized by vasectomy. The operation apparently did the trick. Clawson reported later that he had stopped masturbating. But why this should be so is rather a mystery. Dr. Sharp's "success" with "this fellow Clawson" encouraged the doctor to carry out further vasectomies. In 1902 he published a report of forty-two voluntary vasectomies on men aged between seventeen and twenty-five, all offenders imprisoned in Jeffersonville.

Inducements first introduced

It is one thing to devise a means of contraception, quite another to get people to employ it. In some circumstances they can be bribed. The payment of inducements for vasectomy was first introduced in Madras State (Tamil Nadu) in 1956, where thirty rupees was paid to each man agreeing to submit himself for the operation. Later, payments were even made to anyone who successfully induced a man to undergo vasectomy.

Country in which most practised

India has been represented as the home of vasectomy, the Indian government claiming to have performed upwards of 8,000,000 sterilization operations of which more than eighty per cent are vasectomies. The need for extensive birth control in India is evidenced by the fact that in a population of nearly six hundred

million the population is growing at the rate of up to 14,000,000 every year. In the India of today there are around 120,000,000 married women of reproductive age and the Indian government is pledged to provide contraceptive services of some kind to all of them.

First thwarted by Nature

Vasectomy, normally achieved by tying or cutting the *vas deferens* to prevent sperm being ejaculated in the seminal fluid, is by no means a foolproof method of birth control. The sperm ducts have the astonishing facility, in some rare circumstances, of joining themselves up again, so hard will Nature struggle to thwart efforts to tamper with its processes! Spontaneous recanalization of the divided *vas* has been known since it was first reported by Rolnick in 1954.

First attempt at reversal

In 1886 Bardenheurer was experimenting with methods of restoring continuity between the *vas deferens* and the epididy-

mus in cases of blockage through disease or injury. The first description of a feasible operation is credited to Martin in an article in the "University of Pennsylvania Medical Bulletin" in 1902. Two Italians, Penzo and Gutti, wrote on the subject in 1903 and 1905, while Swinbourne, an American claimed success in 1910 in one of five cases, using Martin's technique. The first British report is a note by Wheeler, of Dublin, in 1914. The first repair carried out for the reversal of vasectomy, rather than in a case of accidental blockage, was performed in 1919 by W. C. Quinby, the patient having undergone a voluntary vasectomy in 1911.

Most serious consequences

Vasectomy, like any other surgical operation, involves a number of risks. What follows must be regarded as quite exceptional and in no sense likely to occur in the vast bulk of vasectomies carried out in a modern medical environment. In the Gorakhpur vasectomy camp in India in 1972 there were at least fourteen cases of tetanus infection. This circumstance led to **157** the first reported deaths due to vasectomy – eight of them were described in the *Times of India.* There can also be a number of allergic reactions. Also, the handling of the structures of the spermatic cord can lead to shock and even to cardiac arrest. In one such reported case prompt resuscitation led to the heart restarting and to full recovery. Mention has also been made of such things as auto-immune conditions and anaesthetic mishaps.

Castration
First practised on massive scale
It is likely that the first tribes engaging in warfare on a systematic basis indulged in castration of defeated foes on a grand scale. It is common knowledge that ancient nations regarded a collection of male testicles as a sign of a warrior's bravery and skill in combat; and foreskins were given in tribute in biblical times to signal the defeat of an enemy. According to Schurig's *Gynocologia,* the legendary Syrian queen Semiramis was the first practitioner of mass castration. According to one theory she had men so mutilated in order to prevent opposition to her female rule – a latter-day Valerie Solanus! Another idea was that she was simply motivated by jealousy. It was said that after having spent the night in the arms of a lover the queen would have him castrated to prevent him giving the same pleasure to any other woman!

Most famous case in 18th century England
There is a much quoted case of castration that occurred in April 1790, near London. A half-wit named James Trotter had sired three illegitimate children who had to be supported by the parish. The Parish Council, apparently resenting this situation, decided to have the man castrated. He was taken by force and castrated, naturally enough without anaesthetic, by the local pig-butcher. No details are given of how Mr. Trotter behaved thereafter.

Most recently practised on Vatican choirboys
We all know that the popes of old used to have young boys castrated so that they would continue to sing sweetly in the Vatican chapel. How many young males so emasculated there is no way of knowing What we do know is that as late as 1890 Vatican choir boys were still being castrated to conserve their soprano voices.

Most famous castrati
During the sixteenth, seventeenth, and eighteenth-centuries in Europe the theatrical stage was dominated by the castrati often immensely wealthy and influential performers. Describing Farinelli (subject of an Abelard book, 1974), D. Charles Burney, eminent eighteenth-century musical historian remarked – "He was able to project the tone to such a length as to incite incredulity even in those who heard him, who imagined him to have the help of some wind instrument." A French commentator, writing of Cresentini, another famous male soprano, observed that this "great balloon" could expand his breath for ten minutes without inhaling! Farinelli became a hero of his time, evoking rapture and adulation. On hearing Farinelli, a woman is reported as swooning in her box, exclaiming – "One God and one Farinelli."

Most famous case of self-inflicted castration
The single most famous case of self-emasculation is that of Origen who severed his own genitals in a fit of religious devotion. Whole sects grew up to practise self-castration and the emasculation of all men and boys who fell into their clutches. In one of the "Dialogues" of Lucian there is a famous tale of self castration. A young Syrian nobleman named Cambobus, ordered to accompany the queen on an extended journey decided to castrate himself so that he would not betray the king en route. He had his testicles placed in an ornate casket which he secured with a royal seal, and then presented to the king. The queen tried to seduce Cambobus on the journey Various rumours got back to the king, and the young nobleman was arrested and charged with adultery. But then – of course – Cambobus played his trump card and the king, opening the casket, saw that he was innocent. Whether everyone, including Cambobus, lived happily ever after, we do not know.

Most famous Greek castration myth

In Greek mythology the sovereign Uranus, the god of heaven, imprisoned his sons as soon as they were born so that they could not seize his power. The strongest and youngest son, Cronos, under the influence of Gaea, his mother, castrated his father and threw his genitals into the sea. Aphrodite sprang from the sea foam that gathered around the severed member of Uranus. Cronos later married his sister

Botticelli's "Birth of Venus" conceals a famous Greek castration myth.

Rhea – and, fearing his own sons, swallowed them as soon as they were born. After Zeus was born Cronos was tricked into swallowing a stone instead. Zeus caused his father to disgorge a series of gods; then he castrated him, and shared his power with his now-disgorged brothers and sisters.

Part VII

Sexology

First liberal sexologist in modern Times

Most writers on sex are liberals these days. There can be little doubt that progressive views are fashionable; they are also, some of us may believe, desirable. At the moment it is relatively easy to be liberal and progressive, a situation which we largely owe to the early progressive writers in the field of sex. Among these Havelock Ellis was perhaps the most significant. In Brecher's nice phrase Havelock Ellis (1859-1939) was "the first of the Yea-Sayers." He contributed vastly to an enlargement of man's view of human sexuality; and he brought to all his work a humanistic sympathy and tolerance which have informed psychosexual therapy and research ever since. Healer and educator, writer and scholar, Havelock Ellis recorded the results of his studies in a multi-volume work, "Studies in the Psychology of Sex", which he published and periodically revised in the years between 1896 and 1928. This monumental work was first published in America, English prudery being too vigorous to allow the book to be published here!

Most comprehensive 19th century study

Havelock Ellis's main work, the "Studies", constituted the most weighty contribution to sexological research in the late nineteenth and early twentieth centuries. One of the volumes was almost entirely devoted to the topic of sexual inversion, or homosexuality. And he felt, for instance, that there were both congenital and psy-

chological factors influencing the pre-disposition to homosexuality. It has been suggested that Havelock Ellis paved the way for the significant sexological developments that were to begin with Freud.

Above: Havelock Ellis, the pioneer sexologist. Left: Alfred Kinsey, who produced the most comprehensive sexological survey.

Earliest sexological surveys

A few small surveys into sexual behaviour were carried out in the nineteenth-century; but perhaps the first of any account was that carried out by P. S. Achilles in 1923. As a psychologist he organized a group-administered questionnaire study of 1449 males and 483 females, all of the subjects from the New York City area. The study was mainly concerned with the effectiveness of certain social hygiene literature in disseminating information about venereal disease, but a number of the questions related to the sexual activities of the subjects. The size of the group is larger than most for that period, but was not broken up into homogeneous groups for analyses.

Most famous sexologist

Alfred Charles Kinsey bestrides the sexological world like a giant. His two reports on the sexual behaviour of the human male and female respectively (1948 and 1953) have no equals before or since in their scope, thoroughness or the richness of their data. Kinsey has been criticized in his methods (so have Marx, Darwin, and Freud); but where is the sexologist in the modern world who does not owe a debt to Kinsey? All serious sexological social surveys, all compilers of statistical and other information in this field, all specialist writers on one aspect of sex or another sooner or later have to acknowledge the pioneering work of Kinsey at the institute he founded at Indiana University. There can be no doubt that the headline-making work of Masters and Johnson is well grounded in the firm empirical approach established by Kinsey.

163

Most comprehensive survey

The first Kinsey report – "Male", 1948 – was based on detailed interviews held with more than five thousand white males; the second report – "Female", 1953 – was based on data gathered in the same way for more than five thousand females. In the *Male* volume it is pointed out (p.6) that "about 12,000 persons have contributed history to this study" Furthermore, this represents *forty times as much material as was included in the best of the previous studies.* Kinsey estimated that no less than 100,000 histories would have been required to complete the project – hence the dedication in the *Male* volume. There are no signs that any such figure will ever be reached.

First female sexologist

A number of the early female writers on sexual matters were mainly concerned with a specific measure, e.g. Margaret Sanger wrote on birth control. It can be argued that such a preoccupation, though praiseworthy, is not strictly sexological in nature. The first woman sexologist in the true sense was Katherine Davis who performed a detailed questionnaire study of 2,200 women in the New York area which was published in 1929 ("Factors in the Sex Life of Twenty-two Hundred Women") The questionnaire was originally mailed to 20,000 women, only a tenth choosing to reply. The survey was said to be confined to "normal" women of good standing in the community, most of whom were graduates. The ages of the women, many of them teachers, ranged between 25 and 55. The treatment of the data has been represented by Kinsey as "simple but statistical". (A much smaller study, perhaps justifying the adjective *sexological,* was carried out by Anita Newcomb McGee from 1888 to 1891; interviews were taken and data compiled with respect to the famous Oneida Community in New York.)

Countries least active in sex research

Of many countries we do not expect sex research – simply because such nations are too poor to fund such investigations (or because they are too pious). Other countries, neither poor nor pious, have a sur-

At the Oneida Community sex was a free-for-all but men practised 'male continence'.

prising dearth of research effort into human sexuality. Of the Soviet Union, for example, Gebhard has remarked – "I know – and only by surname – of only two qualified persons interested in sex research: Milman, a Leningrad urologist, and Vasilcenko, a Moscow psychiatrist." There have been rumours from time to time that Moscow was to create a new sex institute. East Germany apparently only boasts one or two serious sexologists: for instance the survey, organised by H. Rennert, via questionnaires distributed to male and female students in 1963, has been quoted by Kinsey.

First sex institute

The first sex institute was the Magnus Hirschfeld Institute für Sexualwissenschaft, Berlin, and doomed only to survive a few years. In 1933 it was destroyed by the Nazis.

Most celebrated sex institute

It is hardly surprising that, in view of Kinsey's sexological contributions, the institute he founded at Indiana University should be the most famous in the world. Sometimes still referred to as the Kinsey Institute, its correct title is the Institute of Sex Research: it is a mark of the reputation of Kinsey himself that many people seem to be under the impression that the Institute died with its founder. The Institute's primary purpose is represented as the conducting of research into human sexual behaviour by gathering data analyzing them and making the resultant information available to those who need it. The Institute is a nonprofit organization governed by a board of trustees. A high percentage of the subjects being college and club women. In the library there is a vast archive of other sexological and erotic material: photographs, films, drawings, paintings, *objets d'art*, trinkets, diaries, love letters, records, etc. In recent years various police departments have contributed confiscated sexual material. Institute staff have produced books, book chapters, and journal articles in a wide range of publications.

First effective scientific observation of human coitus

For reasons that have yet to be explored in

Masters and Johnson made the most detailed study of orgasmic response ever undertaken.

detail the vast bulk of people are reticent about having their sexual activity observed by others. That such an attitude is not innate is shown by various cross-cultural studies. Any effective scientific project, involving direct observation of human coitus, has to begin by overcoming the reticence in people about having sexual intercourse in public. In a number of small scale projects this was accomplished but it was not until the work of William Masters and Virginia Johnson that the taboo was effectively combatted for hundreds of men and women.

Most orgasms observed in research

Over a period of twelve years Masters and Johnson observed and recorded more than 10,000 male and female orgasms. Dr. Masters began his programme of sex research in 1954 after specializing for many years in gynaecology and hormone replacement therapy for postmenopausal women. He found his assistant, Mrs. Virginia Johnson – now Mrs. Masters – through an advertisement. Their first subjects were prostitutes – eight female and three male – but gradually they collected non-professional volunteers: their final sample was 694 individuals.

165

Earliest empirical study of orgasm in U.S.

The rich tradition of American sexological research began early in the nineteenth-century. As we have seen, by the 1870s it became possible, on a limited scale, to observe human coitus directly. Dr. Beck observed human orgasm in August 1972. In fitting a woman with a pessary to correct retroversion of the uterus she was quick to request that Beck take care lest she experience orgasm, a likelihood in view of her nervous temperament and passionate nature. However, out of scientific curiosity, Beck decided to provoke an orgasm in the woman and observe what happened. "I now swept my right forefinger quickly three or four times across the space between the cervix and the pubic arch, when almost immediately the orgasm occurred . . ." Dr. Beck reported his observations in the "St. Louis Medical and Surgical Journal" for September 1872. An enlarged paper was delivered before the American Medical Association on 2 June 1974 and published in the "American Journal of Obstetrics and Diseases of Women and Children" for November of the same year.

First detailed account of orgasmic response

There were many accounts of orgasmic response before the work of Masters and Johnson. Theirs however was without doubt the most detailed research study ever undertaken in this field. Their findings were published in 1966 in "Human Sexual Response". In particular it was concluded that the long-standing debate about the "clitoral" vs "vaginal" orgasm was largely misplaced, there being only one type of female orgasm no matter how it is caused.

Most ambitious studies of female orgasmic capacity

A number of sexological studies have attempted to relate the orgasmic capacities of women to a host of other factors, such as family background, attitudes towards parents, and personality structure. In recent times the most ambitious studies of this sort were carried out by L. M. Terman. The first involved a large sample of married women (and their husbands), predominantly middle-or upper middle-class in California. The second study was also based on a California sample and made use of wives who were either highly intelligent themselves or married to intelligent husbands. One intention was that the second study would provide an opportunity to cross-validate any findings that emerged from the first. These studies are discussed by Fisher in "The Female Orgasm".

Earliest sexual activity survey by age

The earliest serious attempt to ascertain the age of maximum sexual activity, and the effect of age on sexual performance in the human male, was made by R. Pearl in 1925. This has been termed a nicely analyzed study by a biostatistician using hospital data on 257 older, married, white males, most of them over 55 years of age. They had all undergone prostatic operation. In particular, data from 213 men (average age 65.53 years) – who felt they could recall the frequencies of marital intercourse in their earlier histories – were analyzed. The age of maximum sexual activity for this group was located in the 30-39 year period, a circumstance thought to have sociological (e.g. lack of opportunity) significance rather than physiological. On a limited empirical basis Pearla concluded that the peak of activity "is in the 20-29 decade and that thereafter there is a steady decline." The survey has been criticized on account of its neglect of education as an influential parameter in making rural and urban comparisons.

Most thorough study of female orgasm

The main studies of human sexuality – Kinsey (1948 and 1953) and Masters and Johnson (1966) – drew conclusions largely from statistical and physiological research. A recent publication – "The Female Orgasm" by Seymour Fisher – aims at adding the psychological component to the earlier studies. In addition to giving the most comprehensive review of earlier sexological work in this area, "The Female Orgasm" includes a detailed presentation of Fisher's own research findings. A major positive finding is that the greater a woman's feeling that love objects are easily lost or may disappear the less likely

she is to attain orgasm and that this anxiety may frequently be traced to the dominant socialization practices for women in our society.

Largest pre-Kinsey study group

The only three studies, pre-Kinsey, which approached nationwide coverage in the U.S. were limited to college students. The largest pre-Kinsey study – which just preceded the first Kinsey report –was "The Sex Life of Unmarried Men" (1947) by L. B. Hohman and Bertram Schaffner, based on interviews with 4,600 selective service selectees at military induction centres in New York State and Baltimore. The study was remarkable for its finding that only three or four inductees per thousand reported homosexual experience. However, the Kinsey group later pointed out that "three-to-five-minute interviews ... held in army induction centres were not conducive to winning admissions of socially taboo behaviour."

First statistically based study

Broadly based statistical studies into sexual behaviour are largely confined to the twentieth century. If we stretch the term *sexological,* however, we can find statistical studies as early as the sixteenth-century. François Rabelais (c. 1490-1553) checked the monthly distribution of christenings in his part of France and discovered a peak incidence in October and November – leading him to the conclusion that the first thaws of January and February resulted in increased sexual activity. A later French researcher, Villermé, had reported in 1831 on the basis of 17,000,000 births, that the maximum of French conceptions occur in April, May, and June.

First measurement of coital heart rate

In modern observations of human coitus efforts are made to measure heart rate during sexual excitement, climax, the resolution phase, etc. The first attempts to measure heart rate during sexual intercourse date back to 1896, when G. Kolb carried out a range of experiments in this area. In the 1930s E. P. Boas and E. F. Goldschmidt made similar observations, and in 1950 G. Klumbies and H. Kleinsorge included heart rate, blood pressure and respiratory changes in their experiments.

167

Smallest pre-Kinsey study

Some research studies have been too small to appear as regular references in the literature. Kinsey himself identified on 19 studies of sex behaviour which are in any sense taxonomic. Of these the smallest were based on data gathered by a probation officer who interviewed a hundred boys who were passing through a juvenile court in Seattle, on interview returns from a hundred handicapped females, and on data derived from a study "of 40 superior single men." This latter investigation, the smallest of the nineteen cited by Kinsey, was based on single males between 21 and 30 years of age and for the most part superior college graduates from Universities in Eastern Massachusetts. "Because of the uniformity of the population, the results are better than such a small sample might be expected to give."

Oldest sexist dialogue on women

One of the oldest sexist surveys has the flavour of personal experience and is set in the form of a dialogue between the Chinese Yellow Emperor and the goddess-instructress, The Forthright Female (Su Nu). The dialogue forms part of the I-hsing Fang, a collection of such writings compiled by the Chinese authority Yeh Tehui (1864-1927). Women to be avoided – "If the pubic hair is coarse and stiff, like bristles, or if it sprouts wildly and in different directions, this woman is unsuited. If the lips of the vagina do not cover the Jade Gate, and it hangs below, if the secretions are pungent, then such women are harmful. To have intercourse once with such creatures can bring a withering to the Jade Stem equal to that of one hundred battles with a good woman." Women to be sought – "A young woman is the best choice for such a partner, and she should be a virgin with the Flowery Field as yet unseeded. Her breasts will then be high and not yet milked, and her Yin-essence unspilled. Her flesh should be firm, her skin well-oiled and silky to the touch, and her "hundred joints" should be well-hinged and smooth in their movements."

First study to question women

The Achilles survey also deserves mention a second time as the first American study (1923) to include women in the sample surveyed. The study was carried out for the American social Hygiene Association – an organization engaged in fighting venereal disease, with primary emphasis on suppressing prostitution.

Largest U.K. survey on women

This is the survey published as "The Sexual Marital, and Family Relationships of the English Women" (1956) by Eustace Chesser, hence sometimes known as the Chesser Report. Around 6,000 general practitioners were approached: they were invited to distribute a self-administered questionnaire to their patients. 1688 doctors agreed to co-operate, but 190 subsequently refused on seeing the questionnaire. In the event some 1498 doctors received between them about 18,000 questionnaires. The eventual report was based on material derived from 6251 informants of whom 1474 were in the London area. Only 23 per cent of the questionnaires distributed were returned and it has been suggested by Schofield in "The Sexual Behaviour of Young People" that "the sample was over-represented in the higher educational and income groups."

Most bizarre marriage prerequisite

Many propagandists have suggested that people contemplating the step of marriage should first acquaint themselves with the facts of life. What is generally recommended is that the intending person read some appropriate biology or sex technique book, the more to understand the peculiarities of the opposite sex. Sometimes the suggestions are altogether more thorough-going. For instance, Balzac (in his "Catéchisme conjugal") suggests that "No man should marry before he has studied anatomy and dissected the body of a woman." Van de Velde speculates that careful study may obviate the need for actual dissection.

Most thorough sexo-anthropological surveys

Some anthropological studies relate only indirectly to sexual matters. In Frazer "The Golden Bough" and Crawley "The Mystic Rose", there is a vast amount of both

sexual and non-sexual information. The two most famous anthropological studies that bear *directly* on sexual matters are Malinowski's "The Sexual Life of Savages" and "Patterns of Sexual Behaviour" by Ford and Beach. If any hardy reader is ploughing through the superlatives in this book he will already have met Ford and Beach several times. Their book, as one of the few cross-cultural studies to include reference to animal behaviour also, is perhaps the most quoted of anthropological studies of human sexual behaviour.

Most thorough pre-Masters masturbation study

A number of sexologists studied the effects of masturbation before the extensive programme launched by Masters and Johnson. One of the most thorough investigations of female response during masturbation was conducted by the American gynaecologist Dr. Robert Latou Dickinson whose findings were summarized in his "Atlas of Human Sex Anatomy" (first published in 1933). Dickinson explored theories about vulval and clitoral masturbation and was responsible for introducing, with Robie and LeMon Clarke, the electrical vibrator or massager into American gynaecological practice. Dickinson asked subjects to demonstrate their masturbatory techniques in order to correlate their methods with such factors as the degree of clitoral excitation.

Most important British homosexuality report

This is "The Wolfenden Report", which dealt also with prostitution. The committee, chaired by Sir John Wolfenden, was appointed on 24 August 1954 to consider the law and practice relating to homosexual offences, the treatment of offenders by the courts, and the law and practice of prostitution. Recommendations were asked for. It was largely because of the liberal recommendations of the Wolfenden Committee that the 1967 Sexual Offences Act gave a measure of freedom to consenting homosexual adults in their private behaviour. That the 1967 Act was inadequate in many respects has repeatedly been pointed out by such bodies as the Campaign for Homosexual Equality (CHE).

Most detailed pornography study

There has been a number of studies of pornography, notably in Scandinavia, but also in West Germany, Israel, Britain, and America. The most thorough study of pornography is without doubt the one carried out by the Presidential Commission in the U.S. In 1967 the Congress created a Commission to investigate the effects of obscenity and pornography on the people of the United States, each member of the Commission being appointed by President Johnson. The final report was remarkable in that it recommended repeal of obscenity legislation as it related to adults. The findings – that pornography could not be shown to do harm to individuals or to society – would not surprise liberals, who already know as much. The publication of the report occasioned a brief but heated controversy in the U.S. and elsewhere. The President – by now it was Nixon – ignored the report.

169

Least impressive pornography survey
The least impressive effort to study pornography in Britain was The Longford Report. In the main this report is abysmal – poorly argued, uninformed by a mature grasp of human sexuality, bereft of supporting evidence, etc. We need spend no more time on it here. What is surprising is that this publication should contain a nice little appendix (Appendix V) by Maurice Yaffé as a Research Survey and Bibliography. This appendix, tucked away on pages 460 to 498, is quite out of tone with the rest of the report. In fact the conclusion undermines all Longford's efforts – "In the present state of knowledge it is not possible to draw any useful conclusions which might be applied to this problem and related issues..."

First reading of detailed paper on sexual response
Throughout the nineteenth and twentieth-centuries a growing number of papers on human sexuality have been read at learned conferences. Many of these papers were psychological or statistical in nature and often suffered from a severe lack of hard empirical data. Perhaps the first really empirical paper was first read by Dr William H. Masters in April 1959 at a two-day "Conference of the Vagina" held in New York under the auspices of the New York Academy of Sciences. For several prior years Dr Masters and his colleagues had been studying how the human body actually responded to effective sexual stimulation. Earlier work had been carried out by other scientists: Dr Masters was not the first, but his work was the most detailed, most broadly based, and the most influential in the field of empirical laboratory evaluation of human sexual response.

First study of psychosexual disorders
De Sade's "Les 120 Journées de Sodome" is the first detailed study of psychopathia sexualis ever written and it remains the most complete in its descriptions. This extensive study describes in minute detail as many as 600 types of deviant sexual activity. The value of the work has been acclaimed by medical, scientific and scholastic authorities. And Bloch suggested that this book placed de Sade in the front rank of the important writers of the eighteenth-century.

Syphillis first noted
There is much debate as to when syphillis first happened upon the scene. One theory is that it was brought back to Europe from Haiti by Columbus's sailors in 1494, where upon it spread rapidly reaching France, Germany, and Switzerland in 1495, Scotland in 1497, and Hungary and Russia in 1499. Vasco da Gama took it to India in 1498 and it reached China in 1505. The Archbishop of Crete is said to have died of it in 1506. Diaz is said to have encountered syphillis in 1493. Some writers have suggested that syphillis was present in medieval Europe and "merely flared up in 1494." And some evidence for the existence of syphillis in England is given in C. Creighton's "A History of epidemics in Britain" (Cambridge, 1894); according to this account syphillis existed in England in the first part of the fourteenth-century.

First country to abolish syphillis
There is good evidence that China is the first country in the world to have abolished syphillis. J. S. Horn describes how this was done in "Away with all Pests". Felix Greene has made similar impressive claims for the record of modern China in the area of venereal disease. Thus – "Perhaps one of the most spectacular victories achieved by the new regime has been the virtual wiping out of venereal disease. I visited, in all, ten hospitals in China in city and country, old and new. In each one I asked about the incidence of syphilis. In each it drew a similar response: 'None for two years,' 'None for a long time,' etc. Wassermann tests are required from both partners before a marriage certificate is granted". ("China, the Country Americans are not allowed to Know").

Most popular sex-experiment animal
The fruit fly Drosophilia (also called the vinegar fly or pomace fly) has been used more than any other animal in sex experiments and research into various aspects of

genetics. It was first established as a laboratory animal in America during the first decade of the twentieth century. It proved an ideal subject for breeding experiments since it reproduces prolifically in milk bottles and 25 generations can be obtained within a year. The chromosomes have been observed directly and a wealth of genetic information has been obtained by a variety of experimental procedures. *Drosophilia* has made a fundamental contribution to the science of cytogenetics in general and to the genetics of sex determination in particular.

Erection first experimentally induced

In 1863 Eckhard first demonstrated that stimulation of the sacral nerves produced penile erection; he called the nerves the *nervi erigentes*. Semans and Langsworthy (1938) demonstrated in the cat that stimulation of the sacral and hypogastric nerves would result in a sexual response in the male organ. Dilation of the penile arteries and erection of the penis was produced by stimulation of the first, second, and third sacral nerves. Stimulation of other appropriate regions ultimately resulted in ejaculation of semen. Finally, stimulation of the sympathetic nerves produced constriction of the penile arteries with subsidence of the erection. In 1957 Hotchkiss summarized the peripheral mechanisms in the male.

Hormones first discovered

Of all the hormones – sometimes depicted as "chemical messengers" – only a proportion are connected with evident sexual behaviour. The first hormone was discovered by Ernest Starling at University College, London, on 16 January 1902. He was investigating the origin of the pancreatic juices produced in the intestines to aid digestion. He introduced into the mucus membrane of the small intestine a few drops of hydrochloric acid, whereupon pancreatic juice started to come from the intestine. But how was the intestine stimulated to act under the influence of the acid? Without nerves, it was responding as if nerve impulses were being fed to it. Starling decided that there

must be some sort of *chemical reflex*. With this insight he was on the road to establishing the concept of the chemical communicators, or *hormones* (from the Greek "hormnein", to set in motion or spur on).

First study of hormonal influence on sexual development

Four researchers at the University of Kansas (Phoenix, Goy, Gerall, and Young) performed in 1959 a break-through series of experiments on guinea pigs. Earlier work had shown that when male hormones are administered to pregnant female guinea pigs, the female offspring are anatomically masculinized – born with penises and scrotums. And some experiments had shown that when female guinea pigs are spayed and later given male hormones they display only a limited amount of malelike sexual behaviour. Phoenix *et al* combined the two types of experiments. Pregnant female guinea pigs were given androgens. The ovaries of the masculinized female pups were removed after birth and at maturity androgens were administered. The females behaved much like males. Brecher has termed this the Phoenix-Goy-Young effect.

First sex educator

Aristotle was the main sex educator in antiquity and remained as the provider of basic source material for many centuries afterwards. His philosophical and scientific literary output was so enormous that it has been speculated that many of the works attributed to Aristotle were in fact written by his pupils. Aristotelian treatises on animals, childbirth, etc. continued to circulate well into the nineteenth century, even when it could be shown that a fair portion of what was said in the name of Aristotle was little short of absurdity. At the same time a number of Greek insights were preserved over the centuries. Aristotle describes the persistence of sexual prowess to high ages and points out that acquired characteristics are not normally transmitted. Sometimes – as with the little edition of *The Masterpiece of Aristotle* from the nineteenth- century – authors without any particular merit tried to borrow authority from the Master. 171

Part VIII

Prudery, Superstition
& the Law

"Arrest them all – the laws of decency must be respected."

Most vigorous prude

The modern professional prudes are lazy ineffectual people compared with their great forerunner, Anthony Comstock. Peter Fryer has pointed out in his book "The Birth Controllers" that from its inception in 1873 to the end of 1882, Comstock's New York Society for the Suppression of Vice was responsible for 700 arrests, 333 sentences of imprisonment totalling 155 years and 13 days, fines totalling $65,256, and the seizure of 27,856 lb. of "obscene" books and 64,836 "articles for immoral use, of rubber, etc." Much of Comstock's battle was against the use of artificial contraceptive precautions. The prudes have lost that fight: today they struggle to campaign on other fronts.

Most abused sex book

Perhaps the most abused "sex book" in history was "Married Love" (1918) by Marie Stopes. Based on the unyielding premise that sexual happiness was the right of every person, it offended the Church, conservative medical opinion, reviewers and professional moralists. Inevitably there were publishing problems: two major publishers rejected the book – and Walter Blackie, who had

Anthony Comstock, the world's most vigorous prude, travelled 190,098 miles out of New York City in a lifetime's search for vice.

published her "Journal from Japan" (1910), asked: "Don't you think you should wait publication until after the war at least? There will be few enough girls for the men to marry; and a book would frighten off the few." She is said to have replied: *"What* an idea of marriage you must have if you think the truth about it will frighten people off."

"Dumkopf!"

Most prudish behaviour in modern times

Prudish attitudes do not always result in absurdity. Sometimes they generate a brutal and callous response. The case of Dr. Magnus Hirschfeld, German sexologist, is particularly illuminating. In 1921 he had been attacked by Anti-Semites in Munich and left in the street for dead. In 1933 his famous Sex Institute in Berlin was destroyed by the Nazis. I quote from "The Brown Book of the Hitler Terror".

"On the morning of May 6th, the *Berliner Lokalanzeiger* reported that the cleansing of Berlin libraries of books of un-German spirit would be begun that morning, and that the students of the Gymnastic Academy would make a start with the Sexual Science Institute . . .

". . . an attempt was made to remove for safe-keeping some of the most valuable private books and manuscripts; but this proved to be impossible, as the person removing the books was arrested

. . . The students demanded admittance to every room, and broke in the doors of those which were closed . . . they emptied the ink bottles over manuscripts and carpets and then made for the book-cases . . ."

Books, manuscripts, charts, and other material were destroyed. When the students were told that Hirschfeld himself was abroad, suffering from an attack of malaria, they replied, "Then let's hope he'll die without our aid: then we shan't have to hang him or beat him to death." They later carried Dr. Hirschfeld's bust in a torch-light procession and threw it into a fire. The Nazi report devoted to this "deed of culture" carried the headlines – *Energetic Action Against a Poison Shop, German Students Fumigate the Sexual Science Institute*. The report spoke of the institute as an "unparallelled breeding-ground of dirt and filth" (*Angriff*, 6 May 1933).

175

Most ridiculous prudish society

Until quite recently America boasted a Society for Indecency to Naked Animals. As Peter Fryer nicely observes it should have been "against" rather than "for" – "but the founder was stricken in years when he drew up his will." What worried the Society was the sight of naked sex organs on animals. In consequence efforts were quickly made to design bikinis for stallions, petticoats for cows, knickers for bulldogs, and boxer shorts for small animals.

Most absurd instance of prudery

We could write a book on this one (people have). There are endless instances of prudish silliness in Fryer, Findlater, and others. One instance will suffice here. Many women have been positively repelled by the sight of the male body. A woman of seventy, the mother of seven children, said that she had never seen a naked man in her life; and her sister admitted she had never looked at her own nakedness, because it *frightened* her (P. Fryer "The Birth Controllers").

1972, Lord Longford with a copy of his report on pornography

Most hostile comments about sex

Considering how delightful sexual intercourse can be it is quite extraordinary how many people have been eager to condemn it. For now we will content ourselves with one secular condemnation. The German philosopher, Schopenhauer, reckoned that sex was "an act which on sober reflection one recalls with repugnance, and in a more elevated mood even with disgust." This parallels the view of W. T. Stead who saw the act as "monstrously indecent" and who wondered how two self-respecting people could face each other after performing it."

Most thorough cleansing to follow sex

The religious suspicion of sex is not confined to Christians. The leaders of other world religions have also expressed doubts about the propriety of carnal relations. One example – from the Moslem faith – will suffice. After sexual intercourse or any discharge of semen (through nocturnal emission, masturbation, etc.) a Moslem is obliged to wash himself all over as thoroughly as he can. Until this is done he is in a state of ritual impurity and is not allowed to pray. It is extraordinary the lengths that the pious will go to in order to sanctify gross anti-sexuality.

"Henry, I'm afraid we're through. I've had the lock changed."

Earliest disapproval of masturbation

Many measures were tried to stop boys (and men) as masturbators. Where pious exhortation failed sterner tactics had to be adopted. The most trivial of these were to ensure that boys slept with their hands tied; even adults were counselled by William Acton to adopt the "common practice" of sleeping with the hands tied. Milton suggested a chastity belt. S. G. Vogel had advocated infibulation, i.e. inserting a silver wire through the foreskin, in his "Unterricht fur Eltern" (1786): such a practice was in fact adopted. Comfort has quoted a paper by Yellowlees – "I was struck by the conscience-stricken way in which they submitted to the operation on their penises. I mean to try it on a large scale, and go on wiring all masturbators . . ." If a recalcitrant mental patient tore out the wire, he should simply be tied up. Milton also suggested blistering the penis with red mercury ointment; and cauterization of the spine and genitals were recommended as late as 1905. The most severe cure for masturbation of a man was surely the penile amputation inflicted on a Texan towards the end of the nineteenth century (R. D. Potts, "Texas Medical Practitioner," 1897-8, Vol. 2 p 7).

Severest remedy for male masturbation

We are accustomed to associating the most hysterical opposition to masturbation with the pious souls of the nineteenth century. It is sobering to realize that men and women thought masturbation quite disgusting long before that. In fact the opposition to any form of masturbation goes back at least as far as the "Book of the Dead" (1550-950 B.C.) Later, e.g. in Greece and Rome, the act of masturbation was mildly condemned. In Jewish history it was sometimes punished by execution! In America it has been illegal.

Severest remedy for female masturbation

Like men, women were also forced to undergo spinal and genital cauterization and to wear chastity belts in a vain attempt to prevent masturbation. Krafft-Ebing refers to a girl who "at the age of ten was giving up to the most revolting vices." e.g. masturbation. He adds that "Even a white-hot iron applied to the clitoris had no effect in overcoming this practice." After this sort of treatment the Moodie girdle of chastity, designed for a similar purpose, seems almost mild. In 1894, a surgeon was asked at St. John's Hospital, Ohio, to bury a girl's clitoris with silver wire sutures (clitoral masturbation not having been effectively stopped by means of severe cauterization). The girl tore the sutures and resumed the habit. The entire organ was then excised! Six weeks after the operation the "patient" was reported as saying, "You know there is nothing there now, so I could do nothing." Holt's "Diseases of Infancy and Childhood" (New York), as late as 1936, was not averse to circumcision in girls or cauterization of the clitoris."

Appareils contre l'onanisme.

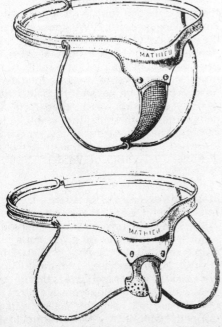

The masturbation belt, an expression of hysterical opposition to selfish pleasure.

First detailed description of chastity belts

Few chastity belts date to a time anterior to the sixteenth century; and a fair number of those on exhibition are thought by experts not to be genuine. A number of well-authenticated specimens however do exist and there are representations in early MSS. One of these can be found in Konrad Kyeser von Eichstadt's military encyclopedia, the "Bellifortis". The MS, dealing largely with Kyeser's military experiences and dated 1405, is now in the library of the University of Gottingen: a girdle of chastity is shown and described. It appears to have been made of iron and could be locked; in appearance the girdle in question is heavy and had little in common with the more elegant later models. Laborde declared that chastity belts were heard of as early as 1350, but he gives no evidence.

Finest surviving chastity belts

The best-known "girdles of chastity" still in existence are generally said to be those in the Cluny Museum in Paris. (See E. J. Dingwall, "The Girdle of Chastity"). One has a stout steel band, covered with velvet, and is adjustable. Beneath the front lock is a piece of convex ivory which, with an oval dentated opening, presses firmly against the vulva. This is dated to either the sixteenth or early seventeenth century. The second specimen is a finer device, thought to be made in Germany in the early seventeenth century. It has two iron plates jointed together at their narrowest point, to one of which is attached two jointed iron bands for passing round the hips. Both the plates are engraved, damascened, and picked out in gold. One carries a design showing Adam and Eve in the Garden of Eden. Drilled holes were provided to allow velvet or silk coverings to be attached. Both belts give abundant evidence of high-quality workmanship.

Best known chastity belt deception

Chastity belts are rare; many collectors are eager to possess a genuine one. Sir James Mann, Master of the Armouries at the Tower of London, managed to purchase one shortly before his death in 1962. It cost him around £350 and appeared to date from the early seventeenth century. 179

However, experts at the Tower have decided that it is a fake and sent it for sale at Christie's in March 1974. A spokesman declared that "It does not seem strong enough for its purpose."

First invention of chastity belt fibula
A fibula closes the female genitals by actually having a piece of metal, ivory or wood pass through the labia. A chastity belt which was really a fibula of this sort was invented by a certain Francesco de Carerra, an imperial judge in Padua in the fifteenth century. His invention was a padlock which "locked up the seat of voluptuousness." Carerra was eventually ordered – on account of various crimes – to be judicially strangled. One charge was that he locked up all his mistresses by means of his fibula. The device was also known as the Bernasco padlock, and it was sold briefly in France during the reign of Henry II. According to one tale, an itinerant Italian peddler opened a stall at the fair of San Germain and sold the locks so quickly that French gallants became alarmed. The enterprising tradesman was soon obliged to flee the town.

Earliest pictorial representation
According to Dingwall in "The Girdle of chastity", one of the earliest pictorial representations is the woodcut published first in the 1572 Bale edition of Sebastian Brant's *Das Narrenschiff* (The Ship of Fools). A woodcut illustrating a poem shows to the left in the foreground a fool pouring water into a well, while to his left is a nude woman seated upon a block and partly hidden behind a curtain. Around her waist is a belt and in her left hand she holds a chain from which is suspended a stout padlock. In other editions of the work the chastity belt is not shown.

First appearance of chastity belts in Europe
There has been much controversy as to when the first chastity belt appeared in Europe. There is little doubt that the idea of such a device was current at least as early as the second half of the twelfth-century. Thus in the Guigemar Epic, which exhibits strong traces of Oriental influences, Marie de France narrates an event which suggests knowledge of such devices. It has also been suggested that a passage in the "Livre du Voir-Dit" of the fourteenth century poet Guillaume de Machaut can be interpreted in this way.

Most recent application to patent a chastity belt
As late as 16 March 1903, Frau Emilie Schäfer, of 26 Rigaerstrasse, Berlin, applied for a patent (Sch. 16096: Gebrauchmuster 30. d. 204538) for a "Verschliessbares Schutznetz für Frauen gegen echeliche Untreue" (Girdle with lock and key as a protection against conjugal infidelity). Writing in about 1930 Dingwall noted that enquiries about the availability of chastity belts were still being made of surgical instrument makers in London – "and doubtless such sometimes supplied."

Most obscene 4-letter word
We all(?) know the four-letter words – *fuck, cunt, cock, arse, shit, piss,* and *fart.* Doubtless imaginative readers can think of others. It is convenient that *dick* has four letters, but such words as *tit* and *prick* do not oblige. Edward Sagarin has suggested in his "Anatomy of Dirty Words" that there is only one four-letter word in the English language – *fuck.* We know what he means. It could be argued that to many people this word has a unique status, a peculiar aura of foulness, and that where other four-letter words may be tolerated, *fuck* would still be beyond the pale. Until recently the word was banned from all dictionaries ever since the eighteenth-century. The earliest dictionary to record the word is John Florio's Italian – English dictionary, "A Worlde of Wordes" (1598).

Most controversial U.S. brassiere ad.
Today we tend to take the brassiere in our stride. Some unhappy folk are still nervous about it and their unease gives scope for simple-minded comedy in West-End theatre and elsewhere. The most controversial bra ad in America was that of the early fifties – those unpermissive times – when the jaunty slogan "I Dreamed I Stopped Traffic in My Maidenform Bra" was coined. The situations varied but the girl was always dressed the same: she wore

only a brassiere above the waist and wandered around with a vacant look among normally dressed people. The idea was that the undressed state was permissible as the girl was only dreaming. Psychologists debated the implications of the ad and what its impact on women would be. Moralists, as ever, fulminated.

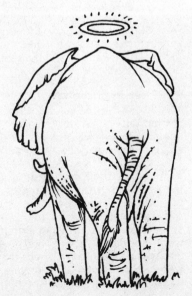

Most sexually pure animal

Animals have been assigned, rightly or wrongly, a variety of sexual and other predispositions. Snakes were thought to be singularly lecherous, as were baboons and other apes. Various creatures have been granted a singular moral rectitude – for no obvious reason. The elephant ranked high among the "good" animals. Thus Pliny credited the pachyderm with every possible virtue: sense of honour, righteousness, conscientousness, and above all a distinct sense of shame: "Out of shame elephants copulate only in hidden places . . . Afterwards they bathe in a river. Nor is there any adultery among them, nor cruel battles for the females." Medieval writers embellished the legend with further details. Albertus Magnus declared that the elephant had no sexual instinct, but conceived and bore in all innocence. In the fourteenth-century one of the first popular zoologists, Konrad von Megenberg, compared the frivolous morals of those animals which "live for their lust without divine worship" with the sobriety of the elephants who copulate only to generate offspring and who after achieving this purpose "do not touch the female for a space of three years."

181

Earliest sex laws

There are a number of ancient codes of law, of which the most frequently instanced is the Babylonian Code of Hammurabi. It has been stressed that the ruler Hammurabi was bringing up to date a corpus of common law which had long before his time been codified by Libit-Ishtar of Isin, by Ibi-Sin and by Ur-Nammu of Ur; and by earlier rulers of Sumer, as well as by Hammurabi's own ancestor, Samu-la-ilum of Babylon. As one example, Ur-Nammu, a king of the third dynasty of Ur, dates to something in excess of two thousand years before Christ. There are provisions in the Libit-Ishtar law code for the penalization of extra-marital coitus. Middle Assyrian laws include the following – "If he has kissed her – the wife of another – they shall draw his lower lip along the edge of a blade and cut it off." In the Code of Hammurabi a man might divorce his wife at will but must restore her dowry and provide maintenance. Both parties to adultery were liable to drowning; incest was punished by death or exile; seduction was punished by fines; sodomy is not mentioned. The later Hittite Code, centuries after Hammurabi but deriving from his code, is generally said to show a marked ethical advance. For instance private revenge, not uncommon in old Babylonian law, is only allowed in one case – where a husband catches his wife in adultery: if the wronged husband thereupon kills both his wife and her lover he is guiltless in the eyes of the law; but if he does not act at once the moment of just vengeance is passed and he must then have recourse to lawful procedures.

Earliest sex laws in Christendom

The early Christian emperors were not remarkable for their lenience in the face of sexual "crime". For instance; pimps, panders, and procurers had molten lead poured down their throats. In the case of forcible seduction both the man and the woman, if she consented, were put to death. In the reign of Valentinian I (fourth century), sodomites were burnt alive. And in 390 Theodosius I proclaimed – "All persons who have the shameful custom of condemning a man's body, acting the part of a woman's, to the sufferance of an alien sex, for they appear not to be different from women, shall expiate a crime of this kind in avenging flames in the sight of the people." The doctrine of Christian forgiveness was quite alien to the early Christian legislators.

Most vicious sex laws

This was a tricky one – not because it is hard to find vicious sex laws in history and today, but because there are so many! Vicious penalties are of several kinds: a person may be imprisoned for life, mutilated, or executed. Of all sexual "crimes", there is hardly one which, at one time or another, has not been a capital offence. One or two examples will suffice. Among the Babylonians and the Zulus (to name only a couple), incest brought the death sentence, as did homosexual behaviour in medieval Europe, and rape in modern America. In old Judaic law, masturbation was punished by death. In Rome the seducer of a Vestal Virgin was scourged to death. According to a law of Jovian in 364, any effort to marry a nun was a capital crime. The list could easily be extended. Sometimes the punishments, at least in theory, did not lead to death. For example, rapists have been legally castrated; adulterers have had their noses, lips, and ears cut off; and concubines in the arms of a court eunuch in ancient China risked, upon detection, being sentenced to having their arms and legs torn from their sockets, their eyes being gouged out, and liquid lead being poured into the open wounds as well as into the vagina and anus. Throughout history people followed their sexual inclinations at their peril!!

Classic sexual psychopath

The case of Neville George Clevely Heath – tried at the Central Criminal Court, London, on 24th September 1946, on the charge of murder – has been represented by Morland in "An Outline of Sexual Criminology" as "the classic example of the sexual psychopath, almost a human blueprint of the type. One of Heath's victims was found with her ankles tied. Seventeen lash blows from a riding switch were counted on the body. And the breasts had been bitten until the nipples were almost severed. A second woman was found with similar breast injuries; and

1890; the scene, Whitechapel, East London. A victim of the infamous Jack the Ripper.

in this case the genitals had been wounded with a sharp instrument (in the earlier case, while the woman was still alive, an instrument had been rotated in her vagina, badly tearing the tissue). One of the ribs of the second woman had been broken. Heath was hanged at Pentonville Prison, London.

Most famous modern British sex crimes

The most famous sexual offender in modern Britain is almost certainly Ian Brady, Myra Hindley or Peter Sutcliffe. When they met, in the early nineteen-fifties, Brady told Myra Hindley of his interest in the Marquis de Sade and sexual perversion. Hindley became more and more emotionally involved. A short time after she became a willing partner in the murder of a twelve-year-old boy and a ten-year-old girl, both of whose bodies were discovered on the moors above Saddleworth. Photographs were discovered of the girl and Brady in obscene poses; the girl had been tortured and a tape-recording had been made of her screams. There is some suspicion that other children missing in the area may have been killed by Brady and Hindley. A third known victim was a youth of seventeen, killed with an axe. Some people have pointed to Brady's liking for pornography as a reason why such material should be banned; others, perhaps more persuasively, have noted that Brady had a reputation for sadism as a child, long before he gained access to erotic literature. Myra Hindley has stayed in the news, partly because she was later befriended by Lord Longford, partly through an abortive prison escape attempt in March 1974. Peter Sutcliffe, known as the Yorkshire Ripper for the extreme and brutal violence with which his victims met their fate, was arrested in 1980. The full grisly details of his horrendous crimes were never made public. He claimed he had been instructed by God to murder women.

Most famous 19th century sex criminal

Jack the Ripper committed the famous Whitechapel murders in London in 1888, before he disappeared without trace. The Ripper claimed six victims (though some writers suggest there were as many as nine), all of them female prostitutes. What **183**

"My client does not intend to remain a peeping tom, m'lud – he hopes to become a top international espionage agent."

is particularly remarkable about the Whitechapel murders was how skilfully the victims were dismembered after being killed. Thus a number of the women had precise cuts in their bodies, organs removed, etc. This circumstance led to speculation that the Ripper had at least superficial medical knowledge; and one of the crimes suggested that dental forceps had been employed. Hardly surprisingly, London prostitutes organized themselves into a "Defence committee against Jack the Ripper" and some of them, friends of murdered colleagues, attended identification parades. Jack the Ripper wrote letters to Scotland Yard. One of the letters is at Madame Tussaud's – "I like my work and I mean to go on with it. You will hear of me and my little games again. I have kept a little of that lovely red liquid in a glass of beer and I wanted to use it to write with but it's become thick like glue and I can't use it. But even red ink can serve the purpose. Ha! Ha! Ha! Next time I'll cut the ears off the lady and send them to the police. Keep my letter until my next success and then publish it maybe. With luck, I'll begin again soon. Good luck!"

Tallest sex criminals

It was found in the Kinsey Institute survey of sex criminals, that the range of median height was from 5 ft. 8 in. to 5 ft. 10 in. "Curiously enough the one group in which tallness would be an advantage in the *modus operandi* of the offence is the tallest of our groups: the average peeper stood 5 ft. 10 in."

Most bizarre Court ruling

The judicial world is capable of absurd and bizarre behaviour from time to time: many rulings have bordered on fantasy. For example, it used to be the case that animals appeared in court, allocated defence counsel, their grunts and whines being interpreted as denials or guilt or confessions. Court rulings followed in accordance with such interpretations. In the realm of human sexual behaviour the rulings have often been harsh in the extreme. Sometimes the judgments seem so ridiculous as to be almost incredible. Here's just one example – in Dittrick v. Brown County 1943: 9 N.W. (2d) 510 the Supreme Court of Minnesota upheld the commitment as a sexual psychopath of a 42-year-old father of six who "was mentally bright, capable, and a good worker," because of the extreme craving for sexual intercourse with his wife, amounting in the year before his commitment to approximately 3 or 4 times a week."

Only U.S. conviction for bestiality

As far as can be judged there is only one recorded case of a woman convicted of coitus with a non-human animal in the United States. It is the case of State v. Tarrant (1949: 80 N.E. 2d Ohio 509), mentioned by Kinsey, Masters and others.

Homosexuality first made non-capital crime

From the time of Henry VIII to that of Queen Victoria, those convicted of the "abominable crime" of buggery or sodomy were liable to be executed. In 1861 in England and 1889 in Scotland the maximum penalty for homosexual acts was changed to life imprisonment. In the 1885 Criminal Law Amendment Act, acts of "gross indecency" not amounting to buggery, hitherto not regarded as a crime, were made subject to two years hard labour: it was under this act that Oscar Wilde was prosecuted.

Most absurd homosexual law

Laws against homosexual behaviour have varied from the severe (e.g. mutilation and execution) to the ridiculous and ineffectual. Homosexuals (i.e. *male* homosexuals rather than females) have often been prosecuted on charges of indecency for simply holding hands or trying to dance together. Perhaps the most absurd law was the one instanced by Robitscher "Statutes, Law Enforcement and the Judicial Process") – the sale of alcoholic drink to homosexuals, or permitting their congregation at licensed premises, was represented as a ground for suspension or revocation of a liquor license, 27 ALR. 3d (1954).

Most recent lesbian legislation in U.K.

In 1921 a new Criminal Law Amendment Act was introduced into the House of Commons as a Private Member's measure. During the report stage, after the Bill had been considered by a standing committee, a Scottish conservative lawyer and son of the *manse*, Frederick Macquisten, representing one of the Glasgow divisions, moved the following new clause under the heading of "Acts of Indecency by females" –

Any act of gross indecency between female persons shall be a misdemeanour and punishable in the same manner as any such act committed by male persons under section eleven of the Criminal Law Amendment Act, 1885.

According to Macquisten the new clause was "long overdue in the criminal code of this country" and he referred with some relish to "an undercurrent of dreadful degradation, unchecked and uninterfered with." Sir Ernest Wild, supporting the clause, declared it "an attempt to grapple with a very real evil." The clause was passed in the Commons on 4 August 1921 by a vote of 148 to 53, but defeated in the Lords.

"It is my duty to inform you that while under surveillance you have been observed to smile at thirteen dogs."

Vasectomy first approved in English law

Vasectomy, nervously seen by some males as akin to forcible castration and the consequent surrender of virility, has often been opposed in law. For a number of years vasectomy has been legal when performed under conditions of appropriate medical control. It was in 1972 that Parliament added vasectomy to the methods of contraception which may be provided by local authorities. This was largely due to the sustained advocacy of the Simon Population Trust.

185

Mrs. Mary Whitehouse, Britain's self-appointed custodian of morals.

James Anderson, Richard Neville and Felix Denis with wigs to cover short hair at their appeal.

Longest obscenity trial in U.K.

The longest obscenity trial in English legal history was that of the Oz magazine under the 1959 Obscene Publications Act. The proceedings lasted for nearly six weeks in the hot summer of 1971. It was also the first major obscenity trial which produced a guilty verdict since pre-*Lady Chatterley* days (1960). The trial was a remarkable affair with Judge Argyle able to make remarks such as "so-called defence experts" – in fact the *experts* including such people as Michael Schofield, Lecturer in Psychology, and Caroline Coon, director of "Release."

Earliest U.K. obscenity trials

In 1663, Sir Charles Sedley, an intimate of Charles II, and two friends got themselves drunk and climbed to a balcony of the tavern, whereupon they removed their clothes and (the reports differ) either urinated on the crowd below or emptied bottles of urine on to them. In any event the crowds did not enjoy the proceedings and Sedley found himself in court. The case is often referred to as the first reported obscenity case, since it showed that common-law courts would, even in the absence of a statute, penalize conduct which was grossly offensive to the public. But in 1708, in the case of *Reg. v. Read,* where the defendant had published "The Fifteen Plagues of a Maidenhead" (said in court to be "bawdy stuff") for gain, Mr. Justice Powell dismissed the case saying there was no law under which it could be tried. In 1727, however, when a man named Curle published a pornographic book, the Attorney-General submitted that the publication was an offence at common law because "it tends to corrupt the morals of the King's subjects and is thus against the peace of the King." The submission was accepted with reluctance: the conviction of Curle's "Venus in the Cloister or the Nun in her Smock" became a precedent for further prosecutions.

Most severe prostitution tax

Brothels and prostitution in general have often served as a taxable source of revenue for municipalities, church, etc. One Pope, Clement II, even found a way of taxing prostitutes after they had died. He issued a bull requiring anyone who had ever engaged in prostitution to leave half of her property to the Church (if she had not made the contribution earlier). Prostitution was taxed in Spain, Portugal, Germany, Switzerland, France, and elsewhere. In Nuremberg in the Fifteenth-Century, money spent visiting prostitutes was tax-deductible. No, I don't advise you to try it on your next income-tax return!

First abolition of prostitution in China

Prostitution has flourished in China over the centuries. Only in 1949, with the revolutionary success of the communists, was a systematic effort made to destroy it once and for all. The ordinary Chinese people have been urged to lead a sexually pure life in the "new China." Prostitutes were "abolished" in 1949: those who had musical talents were trained to be actresses at the Peking Opera, while the rest were sent to work in factories or on farms. In 1953, dance halls were ordered to close and the dancing-girls were urged to

follow the example of the erstwhile prostitutes.

First official order for prostitutes to go topless

Prostitutes were often ordered by the municipal authorities to wear dress by which they could be distinguished. The fifteenth-century authorities of Venice decreed that the town prostitutes must sit with completely bare breasts at the windows. The idea, so the story goes, was that it was required so that the young men would be diverted from the "unnatural aberration" of homosexuality.

Oldest marriage ceremony in Rome

The oldest and most ceremonious form of marriage, the equivalent of the modern Church wedding, is called *confarreatio.* The name is derived from a sort of meal-cake, *farreum libum,* used in the ceremony. Dionysius has spoken to *confarreatio* – "The Romans of ancient times used to call a wedding which was confirmed by ceremonies sacred and profane a *confarreatio,* summing its nature up in one word, derived from the common use of *far* or spelt, which we call zea . . . Just as we in Greece consider barley to be the oldest grain, and use it to begin sacrifices under the name *oulai,* so that Romans believe that spelt is the most valuable and ancient of all grain, and use it at the beginning of all burnt offerings . . ." 187

Oddest forms of marriage

Marriages between young children and old men were not unknown at various times in history, nor – more recently – are marriages between people of the same sex. More strange than any of these is surely marriage between a human being and an animal (which history has recorded) or between a human being and a tree! Tree marriages were prevalent in various parts of India. Among the Brahmans of southern India it was the custom that a younger brother should not marry before an older one. To satisfy the requirement, when there is no bride in sight for a senior brother, he is ceremoniously married to a tree (or to the spirit inside the tree) to allow the younger brother to take a wife. In some instances tree marriages occur at the same time as the marriage of the couple, the idea being that evil influence which may attach to the married pair be diverted to the tree.

Youngest sex offender

An Inquiry initiated in 1950 and carried out in 14 districts of England and Wales covered 2000 cases of conviction for sexual offences, about a quarter of these crimes known to the police. It was found that the youngest sex offender was nine years of age; the oldest was ninety. Most of the sex offenders were between 21 and 50.

Pliny's contraceptive solution – two worms from a 'phalangium' spider wrapped in a deerskin.

Sex first proposed as aid to immortality

As early as the Eastern Han Dynasty (A.D. 25-220), a school of Taoists created the Yin Taoism which proposed a theoretical basis for immortality through sex. The theory and practice were seized upon by the emperors as the key to longevity, if not immortality. One of the Taoist manuals asserted that the Yellow Emperor became immortal after having had sexual relations with 1200 women and that Peng Tsu, through the "correct way of making love in ten to twenty girls every single night", was able to live to a good old age. Peng Tsu thought it a fine idea to have intercourse with virgins – "He ought to make love to virgins and this will restore his youthful looks. What a pity there are not many virgins available... My late master observed these principles strictly. He lived to 3000 years of age ... one cannot achieve one's aim by using one female. One will have to make love to three, nine, or eleven women each night, the more the better."

Earliest contraceptive superstitions

Pliny the Elder (A.D. 23-79) reckoned that if you took two small worms out of the body of a certain species of spider and attached them in a piece of deer's skin to a woman's body before sunrise, she would not conceive. Other ancient and dark-age writers believed that if a woman spat three times into a frog's mouth she would not conceive for a year; and that a jaspar

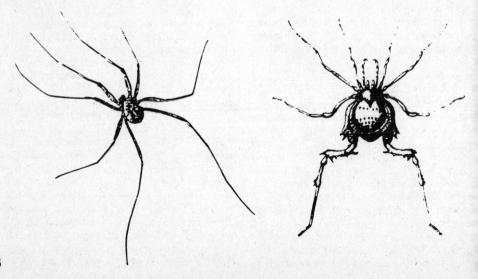

Thomas Aquinas, despite St. Albert's liberal teaching, first branded contraception a vice.

pebble clasped in the hand during coitus would also stop conception. St. Albert the Great (1193-1280), who taught Aquinas, advised women to eat bees as an effective contraception procedure. Aëtios of Amida (fl. 527-565) suggested that a man should wash his penis in vinegar or brine; and that a woman should wear a cat's testicle in a tube across her navel. The oldest contraceptive beliefs hinged acceptance of the efficacy of magical practices.

189

"It's going to be one of those Sundays"

Most prevalent in Rome

The superstitions of ancient Rome were broadly representative of antiquity as a whole. The Roman sages were influenced – as were the thinkers of Greece, China, India, etc. – by the accumulated tradition that sprang from the most primitive communities. Inevitably factors such as sympathetic magic, witchcraft, and the like were spread, in the absence of a sceptical scientific world-view, from one ancient land to another. It suffices to mention one prevalent Roman superstition: that the sex of a child was determined by the testicle which supplied the sperm in question.

Most prevalent in Greece

The Romans derived much of their art and much of their superstition from Greece. In Pliny the Elder there is abundant cataloguing of superstitions common in Greece, many of which were absorbed by the Romans. In Pliny it is suggested that the sap of the flea-wort is effective in securing the birth of boys; and Glaucias ascribed the same effect to the thistle. A pregnant woman could guarantee to have a boy-child if she ate the testicles, womb, or rennet of a hare; and to eat the foetus of a hare removed barrenness permanently. One prevalent superstition was that the hyaena changed its sex every year, though Aristotle had his doubts about that one. (H. Licht "Sexual Life in Ancient Greece").

Most prevalent in Arabic thought

A variety of Arabic superstitions are recorded in "The Perfumed Garden". For example, you are not supposed to leave your member in the vulva after ejaculation, as this may cause gravel, or softening of the vertebral column, or the rupture of blood vessels, or inflammation of the lungs. Coitus with old women acts like a fatal poison – "Do not rummage old women, were they as rich as Karoun" – "The coitus of old women is a venomous meal" – "Do not serve an old woman, even if she offered to feed you with semolina and almond bread." Too much coitus was supposed to injure the health.

Most prevalent among Trobrianders

The work of Malinowski immortalized the Trobrianders. One view was that the male nd female discharges (vaginal fluid) are inked to an action of the bowels. There vas total ignorance of the physiological unction of the testes. Women were seen o have no testes, yet they produced *nomona,* the sexual secretion. The only unction of the testes was to make the penis look proper. In the most important Trobriander myth a woman, called Mitigis or Bolutukwa, mother of the legendary hero Tudava, lives alone in a grotto on the seashore. One day she is asleep under a dripping stalactyte. The drops of water pierce her vagina and deprive her of her virginity. In other such myths the means of piercing the hymen are not mentioned, but it is often stated that the ancestress had no male consort and so could not have had sexual intercourse (Malinowski, "The Sexual Life of Savages" pp. 156-6).

Most prevalent among Marquesans

It is widely believed among the Marquesans that the best part of the menstrual cycle for achieving conception was the period immediately following the menstrual flow, while the period for avoiding conception was thought to be the days midway between two menstruations. Thus the Marquesans had a clear concept of a "safe period": they just got it all the wrong way round. (R. C. Suggs "Marquesan Sexual Behaviour") It was thought that the male would become impotent if he copulated with a menstruating woman.

Most prevalent in Britain today

Superstition persists. In Britain there are still many old beliefs that had currency hundreds of years ago. Some of the popular newspaper and magazine advice columns are deluged with questions and worries revealing a superstitious orientation on sexual matters. According to Marjorie Proops (in a letter to me, May 10, 1972, for which I am grateful) the commonest myths cropping up in correspondence from readers are –

A man with a small penis is always sexually inadequate.

Masturbation will cause hair to grow on palms of hands, make men impotent, women frigid or sterile, cause madness, etc.

Women who never reach a climax are always frustrated.

Women with small breasts are poor risks in bed.

Women with large breasts are always sexy.

Men, according to many wives, are perverted if they take girlie magazines, talk about erotic things during love-making, like oral sex, etc.

WHISPER!
WHISPER!

SNIGGER!
SNIGGER

We would like to thank the following for
their kind help in providing illustrations.
The publishers would be grateful to hear
from any unacknowledged copyright
holders.
BBC Hulton Picture Library
Mary Evans Picture Library
The Kobal Collection
Barnabys
The Bridgeman Art Library
Syndication International Ltd
Popperfoto
International Planned Parenthood Federation
National Gallery, London
The Library of Congress Collections
Rex Features
The Frank Lane Agency
National Portrait Gallery, London
James B. Beckett/Mitchell Beazley
Mary Evans/Sigmund Freud Copyrights
Government of India Tourist Office
Wellcome Historical Museum & Library
Metropolitan Museum of Art, New York
London Scientific Fotos
Dr. P. Morris, Adrian Warren/Ardea Photographics
British Museum
Terry O'Neill/Cosmopolitan Magazine
Jeremy Hammond/IPPF

Cartoons
Several cartoons are reprinted from the
Private Eye Cartoon Library and we
would like to thank Private Eye
Publications Ltd for their co-operation.
Men Only
Frank Dickens
Larry
Michael ffolkes
Hector Breeze
Michael Heath
Tom Johnston
Dicky Howell
Rob Shone

Special thanks for help with the
illustrations to Janice Croot and Negs.

For invaluable help with the paste up
thanks to Safu and Rob.